The Art of Spiritual Living

The Art of Spiritual Living

Joel S. Goldsmith

Edited by
Lorraine Sinkler

Acropolis Books, Publisher
Atlanta, Georgia

Published by Acropolis Books
All rights reserved
Printed in the United States of America

For information contact:
ACROPOLIS BOOKS, INC.
Atlanta, Georgia

www.acropolisbooks.com

———————————————

Library of Congress Cataloging-in-Publication Data

Goldsmith, Joel S., 1892-1964.
  The art of spiritual living / Joel S. Goldsmith ; edited by Lorraine
Sinkler.
     p. cm.
Includes bibliographical references (p.   ).
  ISBN 1-889051-66-7
  1. Spiritual life--Christianity. I. Sinkler, Lorraine. II. Title.
  BV4501.3.G655 2003
  299'.93--dc22
                                                    2003021355

Except the Lord build the house,
they labour in vain that build it. . .

— Psalm 127

"Illumination dissolves all material ties and binds men together with the golden chains of spiritual understanding; it acknowledges only the leadership of the Christ; it has no ritual or rule but the divine, impersonal universal Love; no other worship than the inner Flame that is ever lit at the shrine of Spirit. This union is the free state of spiritual brotherhood. The only restraint is the discipline of Soul; therefore, we know liberty without license; we are a united universe without physical limits, a divine service to God without ceremony or creed. The illumined walk without fear – by Grace."

—The Infinite Way by Joel S. Goldsmith

Dedication

Twentieth century mystic Joel S. Goldsmith revealed to the Western world the nature and substance of mystical living that demonstrated how mankind can live in the consciousness of God. The clarity and insight of his teachings, called the Infinite Way, were captured in more than thirty-five books and in over twelve hundred hours of tape recordings that, today, perpetuate his message.

Joel faithfully arranged to have prepared from his class tapes, monthly letters which were made available as one of the most important tools to assist students in their study and application of the Infinite Way teachings. He felt each of these letters came from an ever-new insight that would produce a deeper level of understanding and awareness of truth as students worked diligently with this fresh and timely material.

Each yearly compilation of the *Letters* focused on a central theme, and it became apparent that working with an entire year's material built an ascending level of consciousness. The *Letters* were subsequently published as books, each containing all the year's letters. The publications became immensely popular as they proved to be of great assistance in the individual student's development of spiritual awareness.

Starting in 1954, the monthly letters were made availiable to students wishing to subscribe to them. Each year of the *Letters* was published individually during 1954 through 1959 and made available in book form. From 1960 through 1970 the *Letters* were published and renamed as books with the titles:

1960 Letters	*Our Spiritual Resources*
1961 Letters	*The Contemplative Life*
1962 Letters	*Man Was Not Born to Cry*
1963 Letters	*Living Now*
1964 Letters	*Realization of Oneness*
1965 Letters	*Beyond Words and Thoughts*
1966 Letters	*The Mystical I*
1967 Letters	*Living Between Two Worlds*
1968 Letters	*The Altitude of Prayer*
1969 Letters	*Consciousness Is What I Am*
1970 Letters	*Awakening Mystical Consciousness*

Joel worked closely with his editor, Lorraine Sinkler, to ensure each letter carried the continuity, integrity, and pure consciousness of the message. After Joel's transition in 1964, Emma A. Goldsmith (Joel's wife) requested that Lorraine continue working with the monthly letters, drawing as in the past from the inexhaustible tape recordings of his class work with students. The invaluable work by Lorraine and Emma has ensured that this message will be preserved and available in written form for future generations. Acropolis Books is honored and privileged to offer in book form the next eleven years of Joel's teaching.

The 1971 through 1981 *Letters* also carry a central theme for each year, and have been renamed with the following titles:

1971 Letters	*Living by the Word*
1972 Letters	*Living the Illumined Life*
1973 Letters	*Seek Ye First*
1974 Letters	*Spiritual Discernment: the Healing Consciousness*
1975 Letters	*A Message for the Ages*
1976 Letters	*I Stand on Holy Ground*
1977 Letters	*The Art of Spiritual Living*
1978 Letters	*God Formed Us for His Glory*
1979 Letters	*The Journey Back to the Father's House*
1980 Letters	*Showing Forth the Presence of God*
1981 Letters	*The Only Freedom*

Acropolis Books dedicates this series of eleven books to Lorraine Sinkler and Emma A. Goldsmith for their ongoing commitment to ensure that these teachings will never be lost to the world.

Table of Contents

The Art of Spiritual Living

Chapter One

The Ministry Within

Human beings can be born, can sin, be diseased, have accidents, and can die without any God interfering or interceding to prevent such experiences. Wondering how this could possibly be, since there is a God, is what brought forth the message of the Infinite Way. There would be no visible universe if there were not an invisible source, cause, or creative principle. There cannot be an effect without a cause. How can atheists ignore the impossibility of an effect without a cause? The naming of that cause as God, Nature, or Law cannot change the fact that there is a cause, and once there is a cause, there is God, regardless of the name given It.

There can be no doubt about God because there can be no doubt about existence. You exist; I exist; this universe exists; and because we did not make ourselves, nor did we make trees, oceans, skies, planets, electricity, or atoms, there is a cause; there is God. Yet, since there is God, how can we possibly account for what appears as the mistakes of nature: man's inhumanity to man; the preying of animals one upon another; the sins of mankind; the horrible diseases of mankind; ultimately the death of mankind? How can we account for those things? It is because the answer to that was given to me, that there is an

Infinite Way, and that we are, at least in a measure, able to prove its principles.

Seek Me

The Master Christ Jesus, explained the evils of this world when he said:

> If ye abide in me, and my words abide in you, ye
> shall ask what ye will, and it shall be done unto you.
>
> Herein is my Father glorified, that
> ye bear much fruit.
> John 15:7,8

But he indicated that if you do not abide in the Word and let the Word abide in you, you will be as a branch of a tree that is cut off that withers and dies. Again in the Ninety-first Psalm, we read:

> He that dwelleth in the secret place of the most High
> shall abide under the shadow of the Almighty. . . .
>
> A thousand shall fall at thy side, and ten thousand at
> thy right hand; but it shall not come nigh thee.
> Psalm 91:1,7

Those who do not dwell in the "secret place of the most High" are the thousand and the ten thousand who fall into all the snares and pitfalls of human experience. There is no way to avoid these snares and pitfalls except by dwelling in the "secret place," by abiding in the Word and letting the Word abide in you.

When you begin seeking in the scriptures of the world, you will find that every scripture reveals this truth: If you seek *Me* and find *Me,* you find life everlasting. If you seek the kingdom of God and find it, you find harmony and peace into which no evil that "defileth. . . or maketh a lie"[1] can enter. But all scripture is agreed that you must abide in *Me* and let *Me* abide in you. You must live, and move, and have your being in God, and you must let God abide in you.

I Can Be Found in Individual Consciousness

Since the importance of abiding in God is clearly stated in scripture, it would seem that the way should never have been lost. History for the past five thousand years, however, indicates clearly that this truth has been lost except to those few who rediscovered it and to their immediate disciples who lived it only to witness it lost again. In my own search, the answer that came to me forms the basis of all Infinite Way work, and that is that no experience can take place in our life except through our own consciousness.

As long as words such as "divine consciousness," "God-consciousness" and "Christ-consciousness" are used without connecting them to individual consciousness, we miss the way. Until we find the kingdom of God within our own consciousness—not a consciousness that was on earth two thousand years ago or four thousand years ago, but within our own consciousness—it cannot exist for us. It may exist for our neighbor; it may exist for those who followed Buddha, Isaiah, Jesus, John, or Paul; but it cannot exist for us until we have searched for and found the kingdom of God within our own consciousness. It is for this reason that the Master was so very explicit:

> The kingdom of God cometh not with observation:

> Neither shall they say, Lo here! or, Lo there! for,
> behold, the kingdom of God is within you.
>
> Luke 17:20,21

The kingdom of God is not to be found in holy mountains, nor in the holy city of Jerusalem or its temple. It has to be found within you.

When Moses received his great revelation, he did not receive it because he was in a particular place, although in the Bible it is spoken of as a mountaintop, scripture always refers to an inspired state of consciousness as a "mountaintop." When Moses received the revelation of God, he found it within his own consciousness. It was not out in the air, and he was not in any holy temple; he was on a mountaintop. It may have been an actual mountaintop; it might have been a mental one or a spiritual one; but certainly he discovered the realm of God, the activity and presence of God within himself. Later Isaiah was led to say:

> Is there a God beside me?
> yea, there is no God;
> I know not any.
>> Isaiah 44:8

The only God there is dwells within you. Later Paul expressed it in a little different way:

> I can do all things
> through Christ
> which strengtheneth me.
>> Philippians 4:13

> I live; yet not I, but Christ liveth in me.
>> Galatians 2:20

Whenever you find a spiritual leader, master, or revelator, one not interested in glorifying himself or building an institution to be worshiped, the same revelation is given to that person: "The kingdom of God is within you."

God Must Be Brought to Individual Experience

The unfoldment that took place within me revealed that, as an individual, I will experience sin, disease, lack, death, war, danger, accident, infection, or contagion, the same as everybody else in the world will experience it. If there is any way to be free of it, it will have to be through bringing God into my experience. How is that to be done? Millions of people are praying and attending church, and still there are millions of cases of sin, disease, and death on earth. How can one help but feel that that cannot be the way?

No external form of worship has brought peace on earth, nor has it at any time in the past five thousand years brought sinlessness, peace, harmony, or brotherly love. The world as a whole has never known peace and purity. A few groups formed around those masters who received the truth and shared it have known it, not the world. The world has had intervals of no wars in some places, but perhaps at no time has there been an absence of war in every part of the globe.

If you look at the world picture in that way, you must either lose hope, give up, and say "There is 'no balm in Gilead'[2]; there is no hope for man on earth; so let us eat, drink, and be merry, for tomorrow we die!" You must either come to that conclusion or you must come to the realization that there is another way and that you must discover it.

For many years I could not find the answer to that problem. I could not find out how to bring God into individual experience, how to bring the comfort, the healing, the raising from the dead, the forgiveness of sin, and the life everlasting that the Master promised. To me these were merely words in a book. Then came the experience that brought with it the realization of the presence of God within, and with it many signs following. This was only a first step leading to the final realization that whatever of God a person experiences, he must experience *within his own consciousness.* He will not find God in a holy mountain; he will not find God in a holy city: he will find the kingdom of God within himself or he will not find the kingdom of God in this lifetime.

Meditation, a Fruitful Experience

After I had the experience of the presence of God, from then on, it was only a matter of listening and being attentive until more and more realization and revelation came, which led me to the rediscovery of meditation. Meditation has been known in the Oriental world for thousands of years. Many times during those thousands of years, meditation was a very fruitful practice. In the last century or two, the fruitfulness of meditation very nearly disappeared from the earth; but with the realization that meditation is the way, the fruitfulness of meditation has returned.

Infinite Way meditation is not merely a closing of the eyes, a stilling of the mind, but is in itself an experience with signs following. If there are no signs following, it is an indication that meditation has not yet been attained, even if hours and hours are spent with the eyes closed. Closing the eyes and getting still is not all there is to meditation. Meditation is a certain specific act which brings forth spiritual fruitage.

If you view the world as I have viewed it, as a world cut off from God, without a God to stop the sin, disease, death, accidents, or wars, and man's inhumanity to man, then you will be able to see how ultimately the experience of meditation will be the salvation of man on earth, how eventually it will restore to this earth, complete peace.

God-realization frees persons from greed, hate, desire, lust, animality, and from the possibility of injustice. Rejoice not in your own goodness or in the belief that you have attained some measure of personal integrity, because only too soon some temptation or other will reveal your own inadequacy. Let your consciousness be opened inwardly; close your eyes to the pictures of "this world"; and within yourself realize this: "It must be true that the kingdom of God is within me. All the scriptures of the world cannot be wrong. It must be true; it must be."

The Activity of the Christ-Ministry

"Man shall not live by bread alone, but by every word that proceedeth out of the mouth of God."[3] Take this passage into your daily meditation for the next six months, so that as you ponder it, eventually it will be revealed to you:

> "Man shall not live by bread alone." Man shall not
> live by effect alone. Man shall not live by food alone.
> Man shall not live by money alone. Man shall
> not live by friendships alone. Man shall not live
> by heartbeats alone. Man shall not live by
> digestion alone. Man shall not live by muscles alone.
> Man shall not be completely dependent
> on the externals of this world.

> I must remember that I live by every word
> that I receive within myself, every word that
> proceeds out of the mouth of God and comes
> to my inner listening ear. I live principally
> by that which is imparted through the still
> small voice within me.

This entire meditation is turning you within. The spiritual life is sometimes called the life of withinness or the interior life. Sometimes the Master referred to it as "My kingdom": "My kingdom is not of this world."[4] *My* kingdom is an inner kingdom and because the Christ indwells you, the Christ-kingdom is within you. If you are to receive forgiveness for your sins, do not look for it anywhere externally, but in you. If you are seeking healing, even while accepting the help of the consciousness of one further advanced than you are, remember to turn within.

Healing is an activity of the ministry of the Christ. "I am come that they might have life, and that they might have it more abundantly."[5] This *I,* this Christ-kingdom, is within you. "I can do all things through Christ which strengtheneth me."[6] That Christ-ministry is within you; the Christ-forgiving-ministry is within you; the Christ-raising-of-the-dead-ministry is within you; the Christ-feeding-ministry is within you.

The entire Infinite Way teaching is based on the principle that you must turn to the Christ-ministry for healing, for salvation, for forgiveness, for food, housing, transportation, for the healing of sin, disease, and death. And where do you turn to find the Christ-ministry? Where but within yourself?

Man Shall Not Live on Externals

Man shall not live merely by external food, climate, and weather. Man must live by every word that can be heard or uttered by the Christ in Its ministry which is within you. The Christ is not a man. The Christ is the spirit of God in you. You need take no thought for your life, for what you shall eat or drink or wherewithal you shall be clothed. Turn to this Christ-ministry which is within you, and when you hear the words, "I will never leave thee, nor forsake thee,"[7] or when you have the feeling of "My peace I give unto you,"[8] your healing and the forgiveness of your sins will have been accomplished. In one way or another the still, small voice utters, "Neither do I condemn thee [9]. . . . Thy sins are forgiven."[10]

The Healing Agency

The word of God which is uttered through the son of God within you says, "Know ye not that ye are the temple of God . . . ?[11] Know ye not that your body is the temple of the

Holy Ghost?"[12] Reading this or hearing it spoken may not always be the healing agency. It can be if it comes forth from the consciousness of one in the Spirit, but nothing can ever take the place of your receiving the Word within yourself. This is your permanent contact with the kingdom of God.

From the moment the contact with the Presence is made within you, you are no longer under the law: you are under Grace. Until that time, you are under the law. You may be under the law of weather; you may be under the law of climate; you may be under the law of age; you may be under the law of food; you may be under physical law of one kind or another; but after you have heard the voice within you, you are under Grace.

Meditation Is an Actual Contact

Meditation is not merely closing the eyes; it is not merely stilling the mind. Meditation is that actual contact in consciousness which enables you to hear the "still, small voice"[13] within you, and be fed by it. The Christ is the bread, the meat, the wine, the water; and the Christ is within you. Therefore, to be spiritually fed you must be fed from within.

Man must live by every word of God. You are not dedicating your life to a man, to a book, or to a set of books: you are dedicating your life to attaining an inner stillness whereby the word of God may utter Itself to you, in you, and through you to others. Man shall not live by baubles; man shall not live by the good will of other people; man shall not live by any human factor, but by every word that he can hear within himself.

Problems Keep Us Alert

The revelation that brought forth this message was the discovery that as a human being I was cut off from God and knew all the evils of humanhood. As soon as an inner contact was made and that Something took over the living of my life, even though some of the evils of this world continued to come near my dwelling place, they were not of the major nature from which most of the world suffers.

Problems come now and then, yes, but each problem that comes is now only another opportunity to go deeper into that Spirit and bring forth more of the Word. Without problems students would just rest back on their laurels and begin to think how good or how set apart they are, all of which is nonsense. Our spiritual progress is in jeopardy in any moment in which we glorify our own understanding or come to a place of believing, "Oh, now I have it." Be assured no one ever "has it."

You can live only one moment at a time, and every moment of your life you are deciding whether you are going to live by the Spirit, by Grace, or whether you are going to come under the influence of the universal hypnotism or mesmerism that binds human beings to the pains or the pleasures of the flesh. Almost every moment of your life you are making a decision, and you may be assured that if you are not returning over and over and over again during the day and during the night to the center of your being for fresh inspiration, eventually you will find yourself living on yesterday's manna. When you begin to live on what you knew yesterday or on the God-contact you had yesterday, you are in danger of losing whatever measure of God-contact you have already attained.

Importance of Periods of Renewal

Why did the Master go apart? Even in his advanced spiritual stage, he went apart from his disciples. He went apart from the multitudes for a week-end or for forty days. If Jesus, in his high mystical state of consciousness, had to go apart to pray at night or had to go apart to pray at noon, would it not be wise to accept Paul's admonition, "Pray without ceasing"[14]? To pray without ceasing means to return over and over again to the kingdom of God that is within you for fresh manna.

I am certainly not in a position to make predictions or prophecies about anyone else's experience. My entire ministry has been telling of my experience, and I will let others tell of theirs. I must assure you, however, that my experience is that if I do not have many periods in the day, and some in the night, for returning again and again to the center of my being for renewal, for refreshment, for Sabbath, I could never carry on this work. I could never even carry on my own individual life, much less the sharing of it with many thousands.

I consider what I knew yesterday to be yesterday's manna. It is only my last God-contact that is the spiritual food I may offer you, not the God-contact I had yesterday, or last week. When I come before you, it must be with a God-contact of five minutes ago, fifteen minutes ago, or while sitting in your very presence. I personally could not live twenty-four hours without constant renewal at the source of my being, constant contact, constant refreshment from within. As I receive this, I am enabled not only to live my life, but to share somewhat with those of you who are receptive and responsive.

Making the Conscious Contact

You have nothing to give to anyone except what you draw forth from the kingdom of God within you, except what you draw forth from the Christ-ministry within you. You cannot forgive sin, but the Christ-ministry within you can, if you make yourself a vehicle for It. You cannot heal the sick or raise the dead, but the Christ-ministry functioning through you can. You must continually make this contact; "pray without ceasing"; turn within.

The time comes when you may need only to close your eyes and immediately find yourself in the Spirit, but again I say to you that there are times when it is necessary to remember:

"My kingdom is not of this world." The Christ-kingdom is of the world within me. I must go within in
order that It may flow out through me. I cannot live
by bread alone, by externals, by reading books or
even by writing books. I must live by every word
that proceeds out of the mouth of God,
every word to which I can be receptive,
not the day before yesterday, but today,
this evening, now, in the middle of the night.
I live and move and have my being by the divine
inspiration that I receive from within me.

This is the purpose of meditation, and you cannot receive
this "bread" without meditation. You can try to know God
through the intellect or through knowledge, but you will not
succeed. You will succeed only as you attain the ability to meditate, to be still, to listen. It might be a long, long time before
you hear God. It might be a long, long time before you feel It,
but time is not of the essence.

The Ongoingness of Life

One of the greatest myths ever voiced in religious teaching
is that man lives threescore years and ten. The life of individual
you never began and will never end. You are experiencing only
one little parenthesis of your life; you will have many more
parentheses. You lived before; you will live again. There is no
such things as a God that ever set a person on this earth and
said, "Now live for a few years until I get ready to end your life."
There is no such thing. Life is God showing forth His own Self
as your individual being. Life is eternal being made individually manifest.

Our life seems to be divided into the phases of infancy,
childhood, adulthood, maturity, and advanced maturity.
Stupidly, we talk of old age as one of those phases, but the truth

is that just as we live through infancy, youth, and maturity, so have we lived many life-spans before this one, and will live many after this one. We are learning not merely to turn from laying up treasures "where moth and rust doth corrupt,"[15] or laying up treasures just to last us for the balance of our days on earth: we are now laying up the treasure of a spiritual state of consciousness that is to carry us through thousands of centuries and is to be the foundation for our eternal existence.

Your Previous Existence

You may ask why you do not remember your previous existences. The answer is that you lived them wholly on the human plane. You had not advanced spiritually on those planes, and therefore you carried no remembrance of your spiritual life. But it will be different from here on. You will carry with you into your next experience the spiritual development you attain in this life, and you will find it to be the foundation for the greater spiritual awareness that is to follow.

Never believe that a man like Buddha, Isaiah, Christ Jesus, John, or Paul came to this earth and attained his spiritual awareness some time between the cradle and the grave. This would be utter nonsense. Nobody attains that degree of spiritual illumination unless he had a foundation for it in some previous existence. It merely comes to fruitage in this one. He may have been perfecting it for several lifetimes.

The spiritual foundation that you are building now or the spiritual treasures that you are laying up in your consciousness now constitute the foundation for all that is to come. Do you believe for a moment that a person receives divine illumination, and then it is snuffed out? No, all that has been given to me in these thirty years or more I will carry with me as a foundation for whatever experience is to come to me whenever it comes.

I am in no hurry to leave this plane, but I am not foolish. I know the day will come when I will leave, but I also know that every bit of light that has been given to me is the light that will go with me and will be my spiritual treasure throughout all the ages to come. Because I have attained the ability to commune with my Father within me, I will carry with me throughout all time the ability to be consciously one with my source, to be fed, clothed, and housed spiritually, so that my body, whatever its form may be, will be a temple of God. This could never have happened without this inner contact with the Father, this inner communion with the Christ-ministry that is within me and is within you.

Laying Up Spiritual Treasures

Every one of us, whatever our stage of spiritual development at this moment, is laying up spiritual treasures. Every one of us is laying up a spiritual life, a spiritual "house not made with hands, eternal in the heavens."[16] You will not do this by outer forms of worship; you will not do this by hoping and praying: you will do this only by inner communion, the actual ability to contact the Christ-ministry which is within your own soul, your own consciousness.

As you have the ability to commune with this Christ-ministry, you will be fed, clothed, and housed. You will discover in the end that "man does not live by bread alone," but by every Word that he receives in his inner ear. Do you have ears and do not hear? Do you have eyes and do not see? Every impartation of God's presence that you receive within you is your bread, meat, and water, even your resurrection.

The resurrection of your body is within your own consciousness, for "I [the Christ] am the resurrection,"[17] and the Christ is within you. "I can do all things through Christ which strengtheneth me," and this Christ is not only your bread, meat, wine, and water: It is your resurrection. It will raise your body from the tomb of sin, of disease, of death. It will reveal to you the temple not made with hands.

Heaven, an Experience of Consciousness

Outer forms of worship may serve a purpose for the beginner; formulas of prayers may also be helpful for those who do not know any better; but always remember that none of these is going to get anyone into heaven. No one is going to get into heaven except through an activity within his own consciousness. "The kingdom of God is within you." The Christ-ministry is within you. In order to attain that inner stillness, be willing to make any sacrifice, every sacrifice. If you have to hide in a corner for an hour at a time and discipline yourself until you make this contact, it is worthwhile. In fact, nothing else in life is worthwhile. Do not believe for a moment that building up circles of friends or relatives, being successful in art, literature, music, or making money is satisfaction. The only real satisfaction is to come to the realization:

"I and my Father are one,"[18]
and the kingdom of God is within me.
The Christ, the spirit of God,
the son of God dwells in me, and I can tabernacle
and commune with this Father within.

Then all your relationships become a joyous experience, all your money becomes a joyous experience, because you know how to enjoy it, how to share it, how to *be*, but until you have that contact within, everything out here is as a shadow.

That is why scripture says, "Abide in me and I in you."[19] "Seek ye first the kingdom of God."[20] Seek *Me* while I can be found. Seek *Me* at the center of your being. Realize the Christ-Self, the Christ-ministry, the Christ-activity within you, and then settle there peacefully, joyously, harmoniously, until one of these days It announces Itself, and then by Grace your life begins.

ACROSS THE DESK

Every day is the beginning of a new year, not just the first day of the year. Begin that new day with the same sincere dedication that is usually reserved for New Year's Day. If we begin every day with that attitude of consecration and dedication in which we lend our minds, bodies, and work to God's dedication, each day will take us a step closer to the one great goal of conscious union with the source of all life and each day we will be clearer transparencies for the divine.

> Let us think of ourselves as instruments through which God's dedication and consecration are made manifest on earth. Each day let us open our consciousness that God may consecrate and dedicate it. Then, to the machinations of carnal mind there will be an invisible sign: "Thus far, and no further." When the carnal mind, the belief in two powers, sees or feels that sign, it cannot get through because God has ordained, consecrated, and dedicated this individual consciousness unto His use. "No weapon that is formed against thee shall prosper," if and when that "thee" has surrendered himself to God's dedication.

This quotation from Joel's book *Consciousness Is What I Am* succinctly sums up the work we are to do each day to be established consciously in the presence. Beginning each new day with the surrender of our life to the life divine ensures a joyous and happy and fulfilled New Year. So be it.

Chapter Two

Remolding Consciousness

When the first railroad trains ran from New York to Philadelphia, their speed was about twenty-five miles an hour. In one of the medical journals of that day, a doctor wrote that traveling at such a speed should be stopped by legislation because the human body could not tolerate a speed of over twenty-two miles an hour and, by continuing such a practice, our population would be killed off. As short a time ago as in my boyhood days, Barney Oldfield made his reputation as a daredevil racing driver by driving an automobile at fifty-five to sixty miles an hour. Recently we have broken through to another dimension where it is taken for granted that men can fly three times around the earth in an afternoon.

Each one of these steps involved a change of consciousness, first on the part of those who had the vision to go into uncharted areas of consciousness relative to time and space, and then on the part of the entire public in being able to follow them.

We were born into a state of consciousness that accepted two powers, that accepted evil as a power and good as a power, and we have become accustomed to the idea that evil is considerably more powerful than good. We are not nearly as expectant of being healed as we are of being sick. We are not nearly as

expectant of prosperity as we are of long periods of lack of prosperity. We tend to succumb to the belief that prosperity is too
good to be true. What is too good to be true? That good should
be greater than evil? Does this seem too good to be true?

Through the newly-discovered mental sciences, there have
been numerous proofs in this century that good is more powerful than evil. There probably are a million or more people in the
world who believe that good is more powerful than evil and that
good can overcome evil. Hardly had this state of consciousness
been reached when along came the Infinite Way which teaches
that we must leave behind the belief that good is more powerful than evil. We must advance to the place where evil is not a
power and therefore we do not even need a good power to overcome evil power.

No Evil Power To Be Overcome

The entire world has been brought up on the belief, first,
that there are two powers and, second, that if we could make
contact with the power of good, it would overcome evil. Now
we are asked to leave all that behind and abide in the realization
that evil, regardless of its name or nature, is not a power, and
therefore no power is needed to overcome it. This is radical,
because every religious teaching is based on an almighty God
that is not quite almighty if it is necessary for us to call upon It
to overcome the work of the devil, or evil. Every religious teaching encourages the reaching out to God to have God do something to evil, whether in the form of sin, disease, lack, death,
drought, or hurricanes.

What a change in consciousness is necessary in order to
understand this new teaching which was given to us long ago:
"Resist not evil.[1]. . . Put up again thy sword into his place: for
all they that take the sword shall perish with the sword."[2] This
religious teaching presented by the founder of Christianity has
lain dormant for the past two thousand years.

Would anyone ever have to petition God if there were not some evil or lack to overcome? Would anyone have to seek the power of God if there were not a power of evil? Would anyone ever have to protect himself with the power of God if there were not something from which to protect himself?

All this has been lost in the human consciousness of two powers. Now we are asked to go back to the teaching given the world two thousand years ago and begin to remold our consciousness to the point where we do not resist evil, try to overcome it, or seek to get a God-power to do something to it. It was difficult then, and it is difficult now.

It was so difficult in the Master's day that he said, "Few there be that find it."[3] How true! How few there are who achieve it! The belief in two powers is so ingrained in us that we not only cannot quite accept one power, but we find it almost impossible to believe that there are no other powers. There is only *Is,* and that which *Is,* is forever. God is from everlasting to everlasting. All that God is, God was; all that God was, God is now; all that God is now, God will be forever. "Before Abraham was, I am.[4] . . . I am with you alway, even unto the end of the world.[5] . . . I will never leave thee, nor forsake thee."[6]

If only we could remold our consciousness to the point of accepting the truth that there is incarnate in us, as a constituted part of our being, the power of God, the power of life eternal, and the power of immortality, we would be able to rest in the Word and behold the divine harmonies as they appear. But no, there is within ourselves an opposition to this truth, not constituted of God, but constituted of the belief in two powers.

The opposition to truth is so universal and widespread that it is almost a part of our nature to accept sin as something so serious or disease as something so powerful and mighty that we wonder if even God can overcome it. The truth is that as long as we look for a God to overcome it, it will not be overcome, because we are dealing only with an imaginary battle, one that cannot in truth exist. It is a battle going on in the mind, whereas scripture says, "The battle is not yours, but God's. . . . Stand ye still, and see the salvation of the Lord."[7]

Appearances Do Not
Testify to Truth

To move from the material state of consciousness to the spiritual involves a change of consciousness. "Ye shall know the truth, and the truth shall make you free,"[8] but the truth cannot make us free until we know it: not merely *affirm* it, not merely *declare* it, and not merely hope that it is true. We must come to a point of knowing, to a point of conviction, of realization, and of discernment in which we realize, "Certainly, if there is a God of infinity, a God of omnipotence, a God of omnipresence, a God of omniscience, how, then, can there be a power other than that of God?"

Nevertheless, that inner resistance to what Jesus spoke of as "the appearance," rises up in us, and it is on this point that we get caught: the appearance. Judging by appearances, the sky is sitting on the mountain and there is no use trying to get across that mountain, so let us stay where we are. Judging by appearances, the sky is sitting on the ocean, just a few miles from shore, so let us not try to go out there, because we cannot get past that sky sitting down there on the sea. Judging by appearances, there would be no use in trying to do almost anything, because appearances testify to the fact that there are powers, not only two powers but dozens of them; there are material powers, mental powers, spiritual powers, psychic powers, and occult powers. One can keep on inventing names for powers from now until doomsday, there are so many of them.

But this has to do with appearances, and the Master said, "Judge not according to the appearance,"[9] whether it is the crippled man, the thief on the cross, the woman taken in adultery, or the boy on the way to being buried. Regardless of the appearance, Jesus' answer was, "Judge not according to the appearance, but judge righteous judgment."[9] We are not to believe what we see or hear, because we have an inner power of discernment that goes beyond what the eyes see or the ears hear.

Spiritual Discernment Sees Through the Appearance

If there were not men and women with powers of inner discernment, we would never advance in science, art, literature, or in any form of good because, judging by appearances, we would always find the present situation too difficult to overcome. Somebody has discernment, and he discovers a remedy for diseases that formerly were incurable. So today the hopelessness of alcoholism is found to be not quite so hopeless because of Alcoholics Anonymous. Somebody had the power of discernment to see what the ordinary eye could not see, and the ordinary ear could not hear. The Master, in his spiritual discernment, realized that God is omnipotence, which means that nothing else has power, regardless of the name or nature of the appearance.

Whatever problem is confronting us, it alarms us primarily because of its appearance. If we could not see it, hear it, or feel it, we would not have any concern about it, but we hear about it and we feel it, so all of a sudden there is concern. In other words, there is an appearance that is frightening. We smile a bit at the person who is afraid of ghosts, not realizing that he is frightened by an appearance that he does not understand. Perhaps some of those persons would laugh at us if they knew the things that frighten us, but that which is frightening us has no more substance or law or reality than that which is frightening those who are afraid of ghosts.

Through spiritual discernment, it has been revealed that what frightens us by its appearance has no law of God, no spiritual substance, no deific or spiritual activity, and no spiritual life to perpetuate it. Spiritual discernment reveals that appearances do not testify to truth. Therefore, appearances must be ignored, while we go within and ask for spiritual discernment and seek spiritual light within ourselves, so that we can "see" through appearances and discern the nature of reality.

In much the same way we might look out on the human scene and see a person who on first sight engenders in us fear and yet, on coming to know the person, we discover that there is nothing frightening about his nature or character.

Our Heritage Is Spiritual

Spiritual discernment always reveals that the *I* of me, which is God, is immortal, that *I* have never been born and *I* will never die, and therefore, there is no appearance that need be frightening, because the appearance cannot change the nature of our true being, which is immortality, incorporeality, spiritual identity or divine sonship. We are mortal only in the degree that we have not heeded the Master's teaching, which asks us to accept the fact that we must "call no man [our] father upon the earth,"[10] that we have no human parentage, that there is but one creative principle, one creator, only One, and that one, infinite, divine spirit. The nature of creation therefore must be spiritual and must be under spiritual law.

Can you imagine baking a pie in the oven and then saying that the oven is the mother of the pie? Just because there is a human oven which plays a part in the production of our human selfhood, should we look upon that as our parentage? But this cannot be true, because even behind the seeds which bring about human conception, there has to be the invisible power which sends them forth. Human parentage is but a process of bringing forth into visibility the invisible life and self which we are. There was life, and there was a self before there was a seed. The seed is only the embodiment of a form.

What a change of consciousness can be brought about when

we understand that our heritage is spiritual, that God is our creator, our creative principle, and that our qualities and quantities are derived from the spiritual source! We were sent into expression by our creator, by the one Father, yours and mine, and our parents are just the human frames through which we were sent into expression. We do not have parents separate from the one Father. There is only one Father, one creative principle.

Letting Old Beliefs Die

The transition from material consciousness to spiritual consciousness consists of a remolding of consciousness. The mystical language for this is that we must "die daily,"[11] we must be reborn of the Spirit. To die daily is to let the untruths and the myths that we have accepted die or be released out of our consciousness. Our consciousness remains just what it always was, only now, for example, instead of believing that the sky sits on the ocean or on the mountain, our awareness of what really is destroys our ignorance on that subject. In other words, we have died to those beliefs. But it is not actually a dying process: it is a letting of that ignorance die out of our consciousness, so that the truth may be born in our consciousness.

As we begin a regular program of training our consciousness to accept one power, and that one, Spirit, and resist the temptation to use that power on anything, because there is no other power to use it on, these old beliefs are dying out of our consciousness, and truth is being born into our consciousness. We are still ourselves; our consciousness is still our consciousness, except that now some of our ignorance has been replaced with truth.

God, the I Am of Individual Consciousness

The teaching that God is outside of us and is a great power is based on superstition. This is not the truth, because there is no God and there is no power separate from our being. It is our consciousness that is the power. There is no God suspended in the air in this room, outside this building, or up in space. It is not a God: it is the God which *I Am;* it is the God which consciousness is. But what consciousness? There is not a consciousness suspended in this room. No one has seen a consciousness out in the air or up in space. The consciousness is *the* consciousness of our being, and the consciousness of our being is God. This would be highly egotistical if it referred to just one of us. The fact that this consciousness is the universal consciousness of you and of me makes it truth.

Most religions set up one person as God, and then leave everybody else dangling in space. This is the height of superstition and ignorance. If this were true, we would have a God and a helpless universe. We have read often enough in scripture about "our Father," but we have not followed that up with the truth that "the kingdom of God is within"[12] us. It is not "Lo here! or, Lo there!"[12] It is not in holy mountains or holy temples, and the Master never said that It was in him, separate and apart from us. Never! He was careful to say, " 'If I bear witness of myself, my witness is not true.'[13] If I set myself up as different from you or if I claim that I have the Father within me, but you do not have the Father within you, then you ought to turn away from me."

Why was there conflict between Jesus and the Hebrew synagogue? Only for one reason: it set up an inscrutable God, one who had to be placated by sacrifice, one who had to be pleased by giving gifts to Him. What happened to all the people who did not have anything to sacrifice or anything to give? Were they outside of God's government?

I Govern My Body and Mind

When we can accept the truth that "the kingdom of God is within" us, that the Father is within us, it is not too difficult to come to the conclusion that the Father is not within our physical form, nor is the Father limited to your form, my form, his form, or her form. When the Master said, "The kingdom of God is within you," he is speaking of something far more important than a body: he is speaking of *us*. And on this point hinges our whole demonstration.

Who are you? What are you? Are you a body with so many pounds of weight or so many inches in height? Is this you? Appearances would testify to that. You look in the mirror and say, "I am so tall and I am so heavy," based on ignorance and superstition, because the body you see in the mirror is certainly not you: it is yours. It would be just as wrong to look at your pocketbook and say, "This is I," as it is to look at your body and say, "This is I." These are not you: they are yours. Actually, you should be in control of your mind, your body, and your purse, and you would be, once you can mold your state of consciousness to accept the truth, "I am *I.*"

I am *I,* and I have a mind. My mind does not tell me what to think: I tell my mind. When a person's mind becomes unruly and governs him, so that he cannot control it, he is mentally unbalanced. All there is to mental imbalance or insanity is the inability to govern and control the mind. When a person loses that ability, he is mentally disabled. It is for this reason that we must acknowledge that I am a being. Even without hands and feet, I would be a being, and this mind and this body have been given to me for my specific use.

This *I* which I am, this identity which I am and which you are, is an offspring of God. It is God-created, God-maintained, and God-sustained. God is the substance of the life which I am; God is the substance of the being which I am; God is the law unto my being; God is the activity of my being; and God functions as my individual consciousness to this end. This is the meaning of God incarnated as man or God expressed as individual consciousness.

God, the Consciousness of the Individual

Your consciousness and mine are the same. I may have filled my mind and consciousness with knowledge of one sort and you with knowledge of another, but that does not change the essential nature of our consciousness. Every child, at birth, has but one consciousness. One child may be trained to be an artist, one to be a musician, one to be a physician, and another to be a mathematician, but all you are doing is molding the mind and consciousness of that child along some particular line. The mind is the same mind and the consciousness is the same consciousness, the same degree of infinite intelligence. Some, through their background, education, environment, and home atmosphere develop lazy mental habits, and others very active ones, but innately, God is the consciousness of every individual.

If I can perceive that there is but one Father, one creator, and that the presence of this creative, maintaining, and sustaining activity is within me, that it is my very own consciousness, then I can walk through life without trying to use a power. You might say, as the Master did, "*I* am: *I* embody bread, meat, wine, and water," not, "I get bread, meat, wine, and water"; "*I* am the power of resurrection; *I* embody the power of resurrection," not, "Oh, I must get the power of resurrection."

One of the constituted quantities and qualities of my consciousness is the ability to be resurrected: resurrected out of the tomb of death, disease, lack, or limitation. Regardless of what form of "death" to which I may be succumbing, my consciousness embodies the power of resurrection. I do not use that power. I realize the truth: *I* am It. It is embodied within me: It is functioning. There is no little "I" to function It, for *I* and It are one!

"I and my Father are one."[14]
I and my creative Principle are one;
I and my God are one;

I and my bread are one;
I and my power
of resurrection are one.

All this involves a molding of our consciousness from the human belief into which we were born to that spiritual discernment which is our right.

Your Consciousness
Molds Your World

Do you know who created your universe? Your consciousness! There is no use in blaming anyone else for the kind of universe your consciousness has created for you. If your universe is not to your liking, it does not mean that you are at fault, so do not attempt any self-analysis. It is your fault only in the sense that you are ignorant of the truth, and as long as you are ignorant of the truth, you are creating a mythical universe for yourself.

For example, it is not everybody in the Hawaiian Islands who thinks they are a paradise. There are those on the Islands who think of them as a prison. Who makes these Islands a prison or a paradise? Who makes of New York a heaven or a hell? New York is neither a heaven nor a hell: it is as good a place to be as any other place on the globe, if so be your consciousness can be molded to understand that the place whereon you stand is holy ground. It is your consciousness that is molding your universe. If you do not have a consciousness of truth, it is molding a hell for you, or degrees of hell.

If you continue to judge by appearances, it makes no difference where you are, because sooner or later, even if it is heaven now, it may become hell later. If you judge by appearances, any heaven eventually turns to hell. As a matter of fact, if nothing else would do it, the monotony would, because even good things can become very monotonous unless accompanied by the power of discernment that can see through the appearances.

I have met people who have left the Hawaiian Islands because of the monotony of good weather. They would rather be in Chicago or New York and have their severe winters, or other places with their comfortable summers. The truth is that we mold our own universe. The only creator there is, is consciousness, and if you have the awareness that God is your consciousness, you will find yourself living in a beautiful universe, no matter where you live geographically. You will build around yourself heavenly conditions, because you are permitting God to function as your consciousness.

The Power of Discernment
Must Be Developed

If you persist in going on in a materialistic frame of consciousness accepting two powers, always battling evil and most of the time observing that evil gets the better of good, that is the kind of universe in which you will live. Most of the time your experience will be on the negative side with some brief interludes of good. If, through the power of discernment, however, you can mold your consciousness to accept the truth that God, your individual consciousness, is infinite, and besides it there are no other powers, life will unfold gloriously and abundantly.

All that is necessary is inwardly to develop a listening ear and be governed by the Father that is within you, not a Father up in the sky, even though the Master sometimes referred to God as in heaven—at least the Bible said he did. You must remember that there were no tape recorders in his day. Not only that, there was no system of shorthand and probably none of his disciples could read or write. No word of the Master was written until thirty years after the Crucifixion, and I am sure that you do not believe that Jesus could be quoted verbatim after thirty years. True he may have lapsed into the idiom of his day and said, "Your Father in heaven." That does not mean a Father up in the sky, but the Father in consciousness. The essence of his teaching was: "The Father that dwelleth in me, he doeth the works.[15]. . . Neither shall they say, Lo here! or, Lo there! for, behold, the kingdom of God is within you."[16]

If you can mold your consciousness to accept the truth that the kingdom of God is within you and then rest back and let this kingdom of God govern your life—not being indolent, but always alert, inwardly listening for the "still small voice"[17]—you will find yourself guided, led, advised, counseled, protected, maintained, and sustained by the power that is within you. You will quickly perceive, however, that It does not go out fighting other powers. Rather, It reveals to you that *I Am* is the power of resurrection. There is no other power; there are no powers to fight. *I Am* the all-power, the kingdom of all-power within you.

Making your transition from a life lived according to appearances to a life lived according to spiritual discernment is entirely a matter of remolding consciousness, letting old beliefs die, so that truth can be born in you. You will then find that you are the same consciousness you always have been, only now you are not governed by ignorance, mythology, and superstition; now you are governed by an inner voice, direction, counsel, an inner presence, an inner power. You do not send It out to overcome the world. You have overcome the world the moment your consciousness no longer fears appearances. You have overcome the entire world in that moment when you no longer fear or hate appearances.

Surrendering Your Materialistic Concepts

In guiding a young child, especially through his early formative years, you must begin with the premise that that child has God-given intelligence. You cannot believe you are giving him any intelligence. You are merely directing him, through education and guidance, to the awareness of how to use his intelli-

gence and what to use it for. If, then, the child is falsely educat-
ed, there is no way to overcome that except to take from him the
falsehoods he has been taught and substitute for them the truth.

So it is that you do not have to die to be reborn; you do not
have to leave this world: you have to surrender the materialistic
concepts of life, all of which are based on the belief in two powers, and those two powers external to you. When you have overcome this belief and have had revealed to you that the kingdom
of all-power is within you and that It is wholly spiritual, then
you have made that transition from being the man of earth to
being that "man in Christ,"[18] or you have made the transition
from being "the natural man,"[19] who is not under the law of
God, neither indeed can be, to being the son of God, who is not
only the son, but heir, "joint-heir with Christ,"[20] to all the spiritual riches.

In religious literature this is sometimes called yielding or
surrendering yourself. You are not really yielding yourself and
you are not surrendering yourself. All you are doing is surrendering your ignorance, yielding up your superstitions, and having sufficient inner spiritual discernment to know the truth.

The major truth is that the kingdom of God is within you,
and that God is functioning as your individual consciousness.
But just so as not to get egotistical about it, in the same breath,
remember that God is functioning as your and my individual
consciousness and his and her individual consciousness. Then
you will be living universally; you will be loving your neighbor
as yourself. It you should never do another thing for your neighbor than to live consciously in the truth that God is his consciousness, that God constitutes his being, you have loved your
neighbor enough to get yourself into heaven. All that is keeping
your neighbor in lack and limitation is the belief that he has a
consciousness of his own.

When the Master said, "Strait is the gate, and narrow is
the way," and when he added, "few there be that find it,"[21]
you must realize that this is not a lazy man's way. This way is

an activity of remolding your consciousness, compelling it to give up its superstitions, its ignorance, its false theological beliefs, so that the power of spiritual discernment within you can take over.

ACROSS THE DESK

In the Infinite Way, we hear much about achieving the silence. The silence of meditation, however, does not necessarily mean that the mind is a blank. Rather does it mean that there is an absence of desire in the realization of fulfillment. As long as we live as beggars, waiting for a handout from some God, we will continue to seek and strive for things or persons.

On the other hand, when we live out from the realization of our divine sonship, as heir to allness, what is there to desire? Is not the ceaseless seeking for more and better things of "this world" swallowed up in the fulfillment of "Son, thou art ever with me, and all that I have is thine"?

Our need is not for things or persons but for a greater awareness of the infinite nature of our being as pure consciousness individualized. Therefore, let us have more meditations in which we contemplate the limitlessness of that consciousness and then live out from that awareness. A study of the following chapters in Joel's writings will facilitate such contemplation and practice:

"Invisible Life Fulfills Itself Tangibly and Visibly," *Consciousness Is What I Am*

"The Infinite Nature of Individual Being," *Practicing the Presence*

"The Indissoluble Union," *The Art of Meditation.*

From the Editor

Good News!

While Joel was making arrangements for a lecture trip to England in the summer of 1955, letters from students in South Africa reached him urging him to give lectures and classes there. After inquiring about the cost of such a trip, he immediately made arrangements to go to South Africa as soon as he had completed the work in England.

When he reached South Africa, he was astounded to find, not just a few students, but hundreds of them waiting for him. It was on this first trip that his baggage was lost, an incident to which he refers in tape 1 of *The 1955 Johannesburg and Pretoria Lectures* and which he used to bring forth a most important spiritual lesson, the essence of which can be found in "This Is a Spiritual Universe" in *The Thunder of Silence*.

All the work given in South Africa was tape recorded and students have the opportunity to hear and study this significant South African work.

The 1955 Johannesburg/Pretoria Lectures

Tape 1: "Introduction to the Spiritual Plane" and "Introduction to the Infinite Way"

The 1955 Johannesburg Closed Class

Tape 1: "The Nature of the Messiah" and "Contemplative Meditation and Healing Work" (beginning)

Tape 2 : "Contemplative Meditation and Healing Work" (conclusion) and "Spiritual Breakfast" (beginning)

Tape3 : "The Spiritual Breakfast" (conclusion) and "The Nature of God, Prayer, and Meditation"

Tape 4: "The Inner Meaning"

An account of Joel's South African holiday, written by a student, can be found in *The 1956 Infinite Way Letters*. The real record, however, can be found in the above listed tapes.

Chapter Three

The Peace-Be-Still of
Spiritual Authority

The first step in our spiritual development and progress
included both a physical and mental discipline. That discipline involved remembering God, refraining from stealing,
envy, jealousy, and not committing adultery or murder. It was
accompanied by the restraints of the thou-shalt-not's-or-God-
will-do-something-to-you. In these early days of developing and
living by a moral code, people were not capable of disciplining
themselves, so there had to be a hierarchy of priests to make certain that the laws were obeyed.

The Body and the Mind
Must Be Disciplined

As generation after generation came under the discipline
of the law, eventually more and more persons learned to discipline themselves, no longer requiring an overseeing power to
keep them in line. Through this discipline their natures were
changed and their desires brought under control. Gradually a
better state of humanhood evolved, which is what always happens when the undisciplined come under discipline. Not only
do they learn how to behave, but their very nature changes,

and they lose the desire and the propensity for undisciplined conduct or thoughts.

In the earliest stage of our existence we are disciplined as to our physical acts, and then later our mental activity also comes under discipline. When Jesus was teaching the principles of spiritual living, he said that it was not enough not to commit the act of adultery, but even thinking about it had to be controlled, because there was just as much evil in the desire or thought as there was in the act:

> But I say unto you,
> That whosoever looketh on a woman
> to lust after her hath committed adultery
> with her already in his heart.
>
> Matthew 5:28

Jesus indicated that first there must be the discipline of rising above the indulgence in an act. Next must come the discipline of the mind, so that it would be incapable of thinking undisciplined thoughts. "He that soweth to his flesh shall of the flesh reap corruption; but he that soweth to the Spirit shall of the Spirit reap life everlasting."[1] In other words if, in our mind, we dwell only on the physical realm of existence, that is what we will bring forth. But if we begin mentally to dwell in the spiritual realm, we will begin to bring forth spiritual qualities. This is all a discipline, and the net result of it is that we become better men and women, more civilized, less materialistic, less sensual, less greedy, less envious, less jealous, and gradually a higher state of humanhood is attained.

Regardless of what good human beings we become, however, we have not yet started on the spiritual path. If we were perfect individuals, obeying all Ten Commandment, we could still be a million miles away from any spiritual sense. Obedience to the law does not make us spiritual. It just makes us good human beings. Let us never forget, however, that there

is little possibility of rising into the spiritual realm if we have
not brought the mind and the body under some kind of discipline and control.

Assuming Dominion
Over the Mind Through I

There is somebody called "I." I am referring now to somebody called "I-Joel" or "I-Anybody." This I-Joel stands behind
his mind and body and can assume dominion over the mind
and body, so that the body cannot do whatever it wants to do.
I am controlling it and keeping it under my government, so that
I know that *I* governs the body, that *I* can take it where I want
it to go.

The great majority of men and women have their bodies
fairly well under control, but most persons still have great difficulty in bringing the mind under control. This, we experience
when we try to meditate and find that we do not control our
mind but that it is controlling us. It is telling us that it will not
be still. It is telling us what it wants to think, and that is usually something quite different from what we would like to think.

There does come a period, however, when you and I do
bring our mind under control, when we realize, for example,
that I-Joel can say to this mind, "Be still. Be still, and know that
I am the boss. Peace be unto you. Peace, be still." I am addressing my mind and letting my mind know that I am here and that
this mind is mine. I do not belong to my mind. My mind
belongs to me. This is very difficult to prove because for centuries it has not been believed or taught that the mind is ours,
that we possess it, that we govern it, and that it is for our use.
But now we know that the mind has no right to dominate us,
but that we have a right to exercise dominion over our mind
and body.

The moment that I realize this, I become more consciously
aware of the *I* that I am. I become more aware of the fact that

there is an *I* separate and apart from mind and body, yet governing mind and body, using and possessing mind and body. There is someone called "I," I-Joel. Now when I think of I-Joel, I do not think of mind or body: I think of myself. Gradually I become aware of the fact that there is an I, a Joel, an individuality, a being, a person, a something or other, and that by the grace of God that I has a mind and a body through which to function, and these are my servants, my tools, my instruments for living.

Furthermore, Joel is not going to live successfully unless he is in control of his mind and body. Heaven help him should he let the mind and body run away with him and dominate and control him. But as long as there is a Joel, and I know that by the grace of God I have been given this mind and body as instruments with which to live my life, I have become an entity, an individuality, a being, a person.

The Source Is Greater
Than Itself in Expression

As an individual child of God, all that the Father has is ours. All the capacity, all the intelligence, all the love, all the being, all the dominion, God has given us. In our infinite individuality we could not be a part of a herd. We are separate and distinct from everyone else on earth, and we have an individual God-given capacity for expression.

To some it is given to be ministers or rabbis, to some physicians, and to some teachers. Each one of us is given some God-given capacity and ability, and that sets us apart in our individuality and makes fulfillment possible for everyone. Was it not Napoleon who said that every soldier has a marshal's baton in his knapsack? Every individual has the capacity of the son of God. Every individual has within him his Christhood, infinite individuality, but he can never attain it until he knows the truth of spiritual identity.

> I am *I*, and by virtue of the truth that I am *I*,
> I have a mind and a body, which I govern and over
> which I have dominion. I am subject only to one
> thing greater than I, the Father within me, not that
> the Father within me and I are two separate beings.
> Oh no, "I and my Father are one,"[2] but the
> "Father . . . is greater than all."[3]

In other words, there is an infinite source of being which is greater than Itself in expression. This, the Master calls "the Father" within. This, Paul calls "the Spirit of God [that] dwelleth in you."[4] By either name, It is that with which I am one, of which I am an emanation or expression. It is this silent, secret, sacred, invisible withinness which expresses Itself as my individual being. It, Itself, is universal being in that It is the *I* of you, and It is the source of your capacity and abilities, as It is of mine. But in Its individualization It is I-Joel, I-you, or I-some-other-you. God the Father is God the son. These are one and the same, but God the Father is Its universal essence while God the son is Its individualization.

So it is then that if I-Joel know that my mind and my body are subject unto me and I am subject unto the Father within, then I am in the position always of being able to live as a listener, as if centering my attention on the Father's infinite storehouse within my consciousness and drawing forth from that infinity my demonstration or individualization of life, including my individual capacities in life. In doing this, I am not in competition with anyone. I do not have to compete with anyone for my success, because I am drawing forth my own individual capacities.

Relying on Infinity, Not Form

If I, as an individual, should forget that I draw forth my good from my own consciousness and should try to draw unto me that which belongs to someone else, then I have lost my contact with the Father and my oneness with my source, and I begin to live out from the forms that already exist. The Master warns against laying up treasures "where moth and rust doth corrupt."⁵ The moment we lay up forms as our treasure and rely on them, the moth and rust will destroy them, and we will not have them for long.

In the same way, when we begin to draw forth what belongs to somebody else, it may become bitter, but when we draw forth that which is our own, that which the Father has given us, there is fulfillment. The only way we can be sure that we are doing this is to fulfill ourselves without having our eyes on what belongs to our neighbor, whether it is our neighbor's business, our neighbor's wife, or our neighbor's husband.

As long as we are trying to draw forth from the world of effect, we are not drawing forth from the realm of cause. We have no need for anything that exists in the realm of form or effect, because the manna falls fresh every day. God's spiritual activity is flowing forth into expression every day, and we do not have to look to that which belongs to our neighbor. We look only to that which is flowing forth through us from the infinite source.

Materialistic consciousness lives out from a limited amount of goods which must be divided, and of course there can never be enough. It is only when we begin to understand our oneness with God that we realize that, regardless of how many there may be, God has enough for every individual, as long as those individuals are learning to draw forth from within themselves.

At one time, when grave concern was felt throughout the country, as it is today, that our oil supply would run out or be inadequate to meet our needs, two things happened to relieve the tension. The first was that tremendous resources of oil were discovered in Canada. But as if that were not enough, a man in California invented a tool that multiplied by four the amount of oil that could be drawn from a well.

Supply, God's Grace in Expression

All supply is by Grace, whether in a universal sense or a personal sense. The cattle on a thousand hills and the earth filled with treasures—food, vegetables, fruit, berries, diamonds, rubies, emeralds—all these are by the grace of God. When supply comes into our individual experience, it is by the grace of God, although we do not always recognize it. But to avail ourselves of the grace of God, it first becomes necessary to understand that everything that exists on this earth, in it or above it, exists by the grace and love of God. God gave his beloved son, the Christ, as our divine selfhood, and God has given this entire earth and all there is therein by His grace and love. It comes into our individual experience only by our recognition of that truth.

We demonstrate supply spiritually through our recognition of supply as God's grace. For example, as we come to our table at mealtimes, we recognize that everything on that table was brought forth only by God's power, not by man's. Man cannot make a tree; man cannot make a banana; man cannot make an egg. All of this has to come forth by the presence, the power, and the law of God. Man can open out a way to bring oil out of the ground, but he cannot put it there. Only God can do that. Man can take pearls out of the sea. But he cannot make them—not the pearls that we know as pearls. All that comes about by the grace of God. The fact that different climates produce different kinds of food must be understood to be through the grace of God, and it is so understood when we say grace at the table. We are not thanking God for having put food on our table or having enabled us to buy it. We are expressing thanks for God's grace in that God's grace is the producer of the food.

God's Grace Appears As Individual Capacity

If businessmen could see a brain on a dissecting table, they would soon realize that the success of their business is not due so much to their great brain as it is to the grace of God that functions through that brain and gives to an individual his thinking, reasoning, and intuitive power. If man would only realize that whatever his artistic, literary, or inventive ability, it does not come from any part of his brain. It comes from whatever it is that is using the brain as an instrument through which it works. A great painting is not due to a man's hand. A hand is a necessary instrument, but it is only an instrument. Take the grace of God away, and what would the hand be? It would be a lump of flesh.

Every activity of life, whether it is in the world of nature or in the world of our own being or body, comes by the grace of God. Without the grace of God there would be no talents, abilities, or great discoveries. Einstein, Edison, and other inventors merely discovered that which God's grace had created or evolved. They could not have accomplished these things if God had not imparted to them the faculty of awareness, of perception, reasoning, and intuition. What would we be without these faculties, and where do we get them?

It is God's grace that gives to this world all that it has, first in the invisible and then in the visible. It is God's grace that gives us our perceptive and intuitive faculties, and the ability to bring them forth into expression and draw them into our individual experience.

The Spiritual Discipline of Acknowledging the Source

Whatever qualities water and food have were not imparted to them by man. They existed before man, and all that is contained in the water and food is there by the grace of God. The fact that we have the power to assimilate, digest, and use them is an act of the grace of God, because anything we could put into our stomachs would stay there forever. It takes a power of assimilation to turn that water and food into our lifestream, and that power of assimilation is by the grace of God. We did not earn it, and we did not manufacture it.

Understanding the nature of Grace is important, because we cannot hope to attain the demonstration, realization, or actualization of supply—whether it is the supply of money, food, clothing, housing, or companionship—unless we can see that in its original essence and nature it is ours by the grace of God. This is acknowledging Him and His grace in all our ways. When an individual goes to the consciousness of God for a solution of a problem, he does not come forth with limitation or division but with multiplication.

Once the mind is disciplined, the body naturally falls under the discipline, and then the mind is free to turn within to that infinite source which is the source of our own being. All of infinity is "closer. . . than breathing, and nearer than hands and feet." If we are composers, we need not stop until we have brought forth the greatest compositions that have ever been known, because they exist within us. If we are inventors, we need not be satisfied with a minor invention. Within us is a God-given capacity and because all that the Father has is ours, we have infinite inventions within us.

We cannot skip this step of the discipline of acknowledging the source, because we will not come to know ourselves as *I*, until we know that there is an *I* which can discipline the mind and body and which can live independently of the mind and body. "I and my Father are one," and that *I* is the Father, Consciousness.

Knowing I *Eliminates Competition*

Before the Prodigal Son became a prodigal, he lived in his Father's house, but the moment he left it he became a nonentity. He became the Son again, however, when he returned to his Father's house. When we live in our Father's house, there must first be the awareness of our identity. When we know that I am *I,* an individual, an entity, a being, we can then realize:

> "I and my Father are one,"
> here and now.
> Where God is, I am, and where I am,
> God is, for we are one.
> And now I can go back to the Father's house,
> knowing that I have meat the world knows not of.
> That meat is my understanding of my infinite
> individuality in God.
> That is my meat, my wine,
> my bread, and my water.
> The awareness of *I* is my supply. I have meat.

If we do not know ourselves as *I*, we have no meat and we would be out in this world trying to get it. If we do, we will get only a shadow, only little crumbs from other people's tables. But if we want the abundance that is our right as the child of God, we must begin to know that I am *I*, that I and the Father are one, and that I have meat the world knows not of. Because I am *I*, I have wine; I have water; I have capacities; I have supply and I have dominion that the world knows not of. But the sons of God know. Whenever one son of God meets another son of God, there is a glint in their eyes, for they know that they have met themselves, another member of the household of God. They know that there is no envy, no jealousy, no malice, no greed, and no competition. They know that they can commune with each other without a single trace of jealousy. No spiritual master is concerned about the students or disciples of another spiritual master, for each draws to himself his own.

This could be true in the business world. Each one would draw forth from his consciousness his own products and his own customers for those products. He would never have to think of depriving another of that which is his. But it all begins with the realization that we are one with the Father and that our capacities are not limited by our education, environment, or personal experience.

Entering a New Dimension of Life

Our meditation will become easier once we realize that we can say to our mind, "Peace, be still." Some of us have undoubtedly seen pictures, statues, or figures of Lao-tzu sitting on a horse backwards, not facing the horse's head but his tail. The meaning of this is that Lao-tzu, the mystic, the man of God, has control of his senses. He does not need to hold reins; he does not need to look where he is going. He is in control of his senses and can forget the human element of control. He is a master and, being a master, he does not have to observe material laws by facing forward, holding the reins, or kicking the horse in the sides. He sits there and contemplates.

There are no masters except those who are in control of mind and body. And if they do not have that control, they are not masters. You and I are masters only as we can demonstrate that the mind and the body are under our dominion.

This body does not constitute me:
this is a body which is an instrument for my use.
I am in the Father, and the Father is in me.
I am subject unto the Father;
I do His will. I do the will of no man;
I obey the will of no man. I look not to
"man, whose breath is in his nostrils."[6]
I look not to the favor of princes. I and the Father are
one, and I am subject only unto my Father
because I do the will of my Father.
I turn within and receive instruction
and light from the Father.

Life becomes a matter of introspection and withinness, letting infinite God, good, infinite consciousness, pour Itself through us, as us, without our having to take conscious thought, but always being obedient to its leading. When the

Master was on the ship in the midst of a storm and command-
ed the sea to be still, he was not addressing a storm external to
him. The storm was within him. A storm is a mental illusion, a
mirage. It is not externalized, and no one can command it to be
still. But we can say to the mind that is entertaining an illusion,
"Peace, be still. My peace give I unto thee."

When you want to meditate, say to your mind: "Peace, be
still. My peace give I unto thee. The Christ-peace give I unto
thee. I bring to thee peace from my Father." As you find your
body becoming unruly, do not be afraid to address the body,
although actually it should not be necessary because the body
is mind formed and if the mind is brought into stillness, the
body will be still, just as by bringing the mind into stillness,
the storm subsided.

When you learn there is an *I,* let *I* address your mind:

> Peace, be still. The peace of God
> be upon thee.
> I live by the grace of God.
> I live by God's government,
> and so, mind, be still.
> Peace be unto thee.
> My peace give I unto thee.

It will not be long before the mind settles down into peace,
because you have asserted your God-given dominion over your
mind, not over anyone else's mind.

With your mind quieted and at peace, now you begin to live
as Paul lived, "I live; yet not I, but Christ liveth in me."[7] Now
you are not living as a good human being, as a clever or bright
human being, or even as a healthy human being. Now it is God
living your life. It is God's wisdom that is manifest through your
being: no longer your mind, your wisdom, or your intelligence.
Now you have died to your personal sense of self.

You must die to your self in order that God can be your

mind, your wisdom, and your love. No longer can you take credit for doing good, for there is no such "you" any more. Now God is living as you, and therefore whatever of good you bestow upon this world is not yours and not you: it is God performing Its function as your individual being.

Then you begin to enter a whole new consciousness of life in which you can never say again: "I would like to do things for the people of the world. I would like to do good, to heal, or to teach people spiritual things." You never will have any sense of wanting to do good, because there will be no such you. That which is now you is really the Christ being you, living you, and expressing as you, and it leaves you with no sense of virtue: no sense of being good, honest, or moral. It is not you at all: it is a something that is living as your being, and all the qualities belong to It.

Give Up Attempts To Improve the Illusion

When you understand what the Master meant when he said, "My kingdom is not of this world,"[8] a whole new life begins. As a student of metaphysics, all that you have been concerned with is the demonstration of the things of this world. You wanted a heart that beat more normally, a digestive or an eliminative system that functioned satisfactorily, more dollars, or you wanted transportation in the form of an automobile or a seat in an airplane, and a room in a hotel. Demonstration was having either more or better matter or more of something of this world, which is no part of My kingdom. But that is spending your energy on demonstrating something that from the beginning was not spiritual, something that never could have been found in God's kingdom.

Your only concern now must be to seek the kingdom of God, and nothing else. As you enter this stage, you will note to what extent you have been trying to improve the illusion instead of demonstrating yourself into My kingdom. You have been attempting to demonstrate more of the illusion: a better illusion, a better dream, more of matter that cannot enter the kingdom of God.

You will begin to stop such attempts because you will realize that if "My kingdom is not of this world," why should you take thought for this world? Why should you take thought for "man, whose breath is in his nostrils"? Why should you take thought for "princes"? Why should you curry favor? Why should you seek more of this world's illusions or baubles, when you can be devoting yourself to the discovery of what *My* kingdom and *My* peace mean. That is the great object of living. What is *My* kingdom? And what is *My* peace? To find *My* peace and *My* kingdom is a greater achievement than the discovery of the atom.

Your World Becomes
the Temple of God

Once you have risen above the idea of trying to improve the illusion, you will begin to see the real meaning of *My* grace. "*My* grace is sufficient for thee."[9] That Grace will not take you out of the world. It will leave you in it. You will still handle dollar bills, and probably more of them than ever before, and you will mingle with people, and probably with more of them than you ever dreamed were in your world before. You will have closer contacts with people than you ever had before.

Few of the distressing and disturbing experiences with people and the lacks and limitations of humanhood will be yours. All these will be swallowed up in the numbers of people and the spiritual love of the people with whom you come in contact, because now you are capable of loving them spiritually. You love them, not for their appearance, for what they have, or for what they can give you. Now you love them the way God loves His creation, without a taint or trace of self in that love. All this reveals itself only when you have entered the second stage of your life, that is, when you have risen above the desire to improve the illusion.

It is strange, too, that the very moment you stop being concerned about supply, supply seems to multiply itself. The moment you stop taking thought about people, they all seem to flock to you and be loving. The moment you stop having anxious thought or concern for business, business has a way of being good. It all happens by your being absent from the body, from corporeal existence, and being present with the Lord, spiritual consciousness. The entire body of your world—whether your physical body, your financial body, your commercial body, your family body, or your home body—will become the temple of God under God's jurisdiction because now your concern is not for the body, but for abiding in God.

Be absent from the body. Be absent from concern about anything that is embodied as form. Do not throw it away and become ascetic, but be absent from it in the sense of concern, anxiety, or fear, and be present with the Lord. This, you will be able to do automatically as the mind functions in stillness, that is, as you have dominion over the mind, instead of its rising up to govern and control you. The people of this world suffer because the mind is not under control. It gets out of hand and dominates them. And then whatever comes into the mind out of the universal mind is thrown at them. When the mind is still, and you are the captain of the mind, then it is under the jurisdiction of God, just as you are. You are no longer so busy fighting your mind that you cannot receive God's instruction.

> With the mind at peace
> and the body at peace,
> I can be one with the Father.
> I can listen for the still small voice.
> I can commune and tabernacle with God.
> I can be absent from the body
> and present with the Lord.

And that is the secret of the highest form of life — the spiritual or mystical life.

Across The Desk

Many students of the Infinite Way enjoy happy, harmonious, and prosperous lives through their study and application of spiritual principles. Students, however, must be alert not to fall into the trap of ease and comfort in good humanhood. This stops spiritual progress abruptly. The student, in his daily study and meditation, must see beyond the pairs of opposites and be willing to release good humanhood as quickly as he seeks to release the bad.

The practice of impersonalization will help to keep the student from falling into the trap of resting in good humanhood. Impersonalization is the realization that neither the good nor the bad is personal to him in his experience. The bad is a universal mesmerism imposed and is without cause, effect, condition, or person to act through or upon. The outer good must be understood as the effect of a greater awareness of God and not as a personal condition. The student must continually perceive the nature of error as the carnal mind, which has no real existence. Thus freed of the belief in a power apart from God, the joyous, impersonal nature of God-being becomes his experience, enabling the student to function as a witness and a beholder of the glory of God expressing as his life.

Tape Recorded Excerpts
Prepared by the Editor

So many times Joel stresses the importance of persistence, but in the Johannesburg work this necessary discipline in following a spiritual way of life is brought out with special clarity. The Infinite Way of life is a constant dwelling in the truth of omnipresence and omnipotence until the consciousness comes that there is nothing other than the One, hence nothing to battle or overcome.

"Persistence"

"When God is accepted as one presence, one power, without an opposite or opposition, when God is accepted as the Infinite and the Only, in that moment do the so-called errors of sense begin to drop away. As long as we are battling these discords of earth, we multiply them. . . . There is that principle in scripture of not fighting evil, not fighting it and not pulling up the weeds, but letting the tares and the wheat grow together, and then in their due time the tares fall away.

"The very moment you accept, even if you accept it intellectually—even if you can only agree with your mind that that makes sense—that God is one and God is all and God is infinite, therefore you do not have to fear what mortal man or mortal mind or mortal condition can do to you, if only you can accept that as an intellectual premise and hold to it consistently for a week or a month, or for six weeks or nine weeks, you will find that the hard shell of the errors in your experience is beginning to crumble. . . . Hold to this truth in your consciousness:

> God is one, and besides Him, there is no other.
> God is the only power; therefore, I do not have to
> fight the power of man, the power of beasts, the
> power of condition, the power of circumstance.
> I accept God as infinite being.

"Watch what a few weeks of consistent holding to that truth will do to whatever hard crust of error is disturbing the harmony of your existence."

Joel S. Goldsmith, "Introduction to the Spiritual Plane,"
The 1955 Johannesburg Pretoria Lectures.

Chapter Four

The Hidden Kingdom

We have been erroneously taught to pray to God for things like money, automobiles, homes, companionship, marriage, or divorce, and that, under certain circumstances, God will grant our requests. We have also been taught that we can pray for peace on earth, while at the same time our armies are out fighting, using the most sophisticated and deadly weapons.

When the metaphysical movement began, this type of petitionary prayer was changed into an affirmative type by which we hoped to accomplish better results. We became convinced that if we just made the right declarations, we not only could get an automobile, but we could name the particular make of car we wanted. We not only could get a home, but we could select the climate in which the home should be located. We could pray for a wife or a husband and could even pray for a divorce. All things, we were told, are possible to God, if we just used the right combination of words and thoughts.

To a God of Spirit, Pray Only for Spiritual Things

Certainly, this new type of prayer has not been any more successful than the old form of prayer. One element was forgotten, one! "God is a spirit: and they that worship him must worship him in spirit and in truth."[1] We must take no thought for anything of a material nature, not for what we should eat, what we should drink, or with what we should be clothed. That includes taking no thought for money, because it is money that brings us food, clothing, and housing.

When we pray, let it be "Give us this day our daily bread,"[2] meaning, give us Grace for today, give us Thy substance, Thy truth, Thy word. "Man shall not live by bread alone, but by every word that proceedeth out of the mouth of God."[3] So we must pray for that Word. The Word is incorporeal and spiritual, but somehow, when we pray for the Word, the bread comes, and the meat, the wine, the water, the clothing, and the housing.

God is spirit, and if we ask anything of God—not in the name of a department store or an automobile dealer—if we ask anything in the name of the Christ, in the nature of the Christ, it will be granted unto us. The important condition is to ask in the name of the Christ. When we do this, we can see how unbelievably well it works. We can ask anything of God that is of the nature of spirit or in the nature of the incorporeal. We must take the word *incorporeal* into our consciousness and hold it close: incorporeal, without physical body.

The key to effectual prayer is to pray for anything we want that does not have a physical body or form, that is, corporeality. We have a right to pray for anything in the spiritual realm: spiritual light, spiritual wisdom, spiritual truth, spiritual bread, spiritual wine, spiritual water, spiritual resurrection, anything in the nature of incorporeal substance, being, or form. As we do that, our prayers will be answered and will appear in the tangible form of food, clothing, housing, and companionship, and all the things that have corporeal form.

It is strange but true that God knows nothing of material clothing or housing. As far as God is concerned, I am sure that He does not see any need for us to wear clothes or to be housed.

Angels are neither clothed nor housed, and we are really angels. But clothing, housing, and material food are part of our particular need at our level of consciousness, and since God does not come down to this level of consciousness, we have to raise ourselves up above human consciousness into God-consciousness. When we come down again into the world, we find what we need in forms understandable to us.

No one knows how God functions. It is not possible to understand how spirit operates. Moses never revealed how his prayer resulted in manna falling from the sky; the Master never revealed how prayer turns itself into loaves and fishes, because no one knows how "the effectual fervent prayer of a righteous man"[4] operates. We only know that it does operate. As long as we do not pray for the Red Sea to open and instead pray for the realization of omnipresence, our particular Red Sea will open, but we never will discover how it happens, because it happens behind the scenes.

The Greater the Degree of Our Giving, the Greater the Prayer

We cannot pray to God for healing, even though for thousands of years there have been people who have done so. But the healing rarely happens. From a survey of the hundred thousand persons who went to Lourdes in one year, it was learned that fifteen received healing. That could not have been because God had anything against 99,985. What it really means is that the fifteen who were healed had consciously or unconsciously discovered the secret of prayer. When those hundred thousand cases were investigated, it was found that the fifteen people who were healed went to Lourdes and prayed for somebody they thought was worse off than themselves and were willing to give up their own hope of well-being in order to pray that somebody else might have life. In doing that, they discovered the secret of prayer.

Prayer is not a receiving: it is a giving. The greater the degree of our giving, the greater the degree of our prayer. It is interesting to note that if we stop praying for our health and instead pray that God may reveal Himself and that God's grace and the way of God may be revealed to us, then when our prayer is answered, it has a way of revealing that our body has been healed. How the two come together, I do not know, and I have never met anyone who did, but it is a fact that it happens once we stop trying to pray to Spirit to do something to corporeality, once we leave the realm of corporeality and lift ourselves in prayer up to the kingdom of God.

Seek "My Kingdom" and Not More or Better "This World"

Reveal Thyself. Father,
I am praying in the name of Spirit.
Reveal to me the kingdom about which the
Master spoke, taught, and prayed.
Reveal to me Thy kingdom. I am not asking
for anything in this world. I am willing to
leave this world. Only reveal to me
Thy kingdom.

What is this "Thy kingdom"? What is this great consciousness to which the Master devoted three years of preaching and teaching? What is this spiritual kingdom? Heretofore we have lived our whole life trying to make this world better or trying to get God to make this world better, while all the time the Master was telling us, "My kingdom is not of this world."[5] All our life we have been trying to find the kind of peace this world can give: a healthier body, a wealthier pocketbook; and the Master was saying, "My peace I give unto you, not as the world giveth, give I unto you."[6] It is a peace of a different nature, and we have not been curious enough to find out what that peace is. We continue to seek only the peace and the kingdom of this world, instead of listening to the Master who said, "Follow me,"[7] meaning, "Leave this world. Leave all. 'He that loveth father or mother more than me is not worthy of me.'"[8] It may be considered too difficult or too abstract to live that kind of a life, but how do we know what we are going to find until we attain it?

A man who had lost his position wrote me, kicking against God, prayer, and truth because he had lost his job, even though he had been very specific in his prayers that this particular employment be continued. I wrote to him that if he actually believed in a God of omniscience, omnipotence, and omnipresence, he must also believe that God must have moved him out of that position with something better in mind. But his attitude was, "Let me hold onto yesterday's manna. Do not let me trust God for tomorrow. I know what I have now, and I am not taking any chances of losing it, not even for the kingdom of God."

We should be willing to stop praying for more of what we already have and say to ourselves, "I really wonder what I would find if I ever entered *My* kingdom, the Christ-kingdom, if I ever received the grace of *My* peace, the Christ-peace. I wonder what it is like, what it would consist of, what kind of a world it would be."

The spiritual path is a life of adventure. We really do not know how much of an adventure it is until we arrive at that place where we are willing to stop demonstrating more of what we already have and seek for a realm and a peace heretofore unknown to us, willingly recognizing, "All right, if it is of God and a part of the promised Christ-revelation, it must be good. Then I can abandon my prayers for more money, a better position, a better home, or a better marriage. I can abandon all my prayers for any earthly thing and pray only: 'Thy kingdom come. Thy will be done.'[9] Thy grace be established in me. Now let me steadfastly look away from this human picture with all its promised good and discover what happens when I enter that spiritual kingdom."

Discovering the Kingdom Through Spiritual Discernment

The kingdom of God is not far away from any one of us: the kingdom of God is within us. We do not have to be a Byrd, a Shackleton, or any great explorer to find this kingdom; we do not even have to be a Sir Galahad seeking far and wide for the Holy Grail. We can stay in our home or place of work and search for this great kingdom, because it is always where we are. "The place whereon thou standest is holy ground,"[10] because the kingdom of God is there. We do not have to go anywhere to find it. It is "without money and without price."[11] We do not need money to seek for it; it is closer to us than our very breath. But one thing, and only one, is necessary: to stop holding onto our dependence on mother, brother, sister, or father, even for their companionship, and to be willing, if necessary, to lose all for the greater gain of the kingdom of God.

There is the rub! Sometimes we have to lose our friends. Sometimes we have to lose our relatives. Very often we have to lose all our friends at church. They have a way of leaving us when we become what appears odd to them. From their standpoint, we are odd to want the Christ-kingdom. They do not see anything wrong with this world. To seek the Christ-kingdom is to seek that which is humanly unknown. The Christ-kingdom has never been known to anyone when he was in the three-dimensional mind, that is, in the human thinking mind.

The kingdom of God can be discovered only through the soul-sense or soul-capacity. Spiritual discernment is another term for it. We either receive it by Grace or develop an inner discernment that the people of this world cannot know. It is the discernment that Peter had when he looked at a man in a Hebrew robe, a member of the Hebrew synagogue, and a preacher on its platform, and said, "Thou art the Christ."[12] The Master responded with, "Flesh and blood hath not revealed it unto thee"[13]—meaning not your human mind, not your education or your lack of it, but your spiritual discernment. It is spiritual capacity that reveals true identity.

When we call upon a practitioner with a developed consciousness for help, that practitioner may see a person in sin, sickness, or poverty, because that is what we may be showing forth to the physical eyes. But when that practitioner closes his eyes and goes within to his developed soul-capacity or spiritual discernment, he sees or feels our spiritual identity.

It is possible to go into a prison—I say this from experience—talk to a murderer, witness his spiritual identity, and bring him forth from prison pardoned. It is possible to look at the sick, the sinning, and the dying, and if we catch a clear enough vision of spiritual identity, that person can be raised up into health or wholeness. We cannot do that by studying books and relying on what they say. That is just mental hocus-pocus, abracadabra. If we study the spiritual message in the books long enough to build a spiritual consciousness, however, we will have the consciousness that heals the sick and forgives the sinning. It is as easy to forgive sinners, if not easier, than it is to heal the sick. The sick usually have a sense of self-righteousness, an I-do-not-deserve-this attitude, whereas the sinner has a sense of humility that says, "Humanly, I do not deserve any better." In that humility we can lift him up. Self-righteousness shuts out from us the benefit of spiritual vision.

Humility, Requisite

Spiritual vision comes forth as fruitage through humility. The person who is acting as a spiritual teacher or practitioner must have the humility to know that no part of his humanhood, not even including all his intellectual attainments, is a healing agency. If there is any healing, it is the presence of God within. Without that humility there will be no healing.

On the other hand, for the best results, the patient should have that sense of humility that knows that he has been living on a material plane of existence and has brought forth a materi-al sense of health or sickness. "He that soweth to his flesh shall of the flesh reap corruption."[14] If we live by a material standard of life, even if it is a good one, we will bring forth corruption, because it is the nature of all material creation to end up as cor-ruption or destruction.

At least let us have the humility to know that we were born and brought up on a material plane of existence. Now we are struggling to come out of it and to rise into that higher altitude of prayer: Father, I am not praying for any earthly thing or condition. What is this hidden kingdom? What is this hidden manna?

The Meat the World Knows Not Of

One of the Master's statements that has been so precious to me and so helpful in bringing forth harmony at every level of life is this: "I have meat to eat that ye know not of."[15] This pas-sage is reminding me that I have within me a little corner, a *something* which the world cannot see. My mother could not see It; my wife cannot see It. It is a corner hidden within me, and that is where my faith, my hope, and my reliance are. I am not looking to "man, whose breath is in his nostrils."[16] I am not looking to improved physical conditions. I am not looking to some form of world government such as the United Nations. I am not looking to some dictator to become loving, nor am I looking to anybody to defeat him.

I have a meat, I have a substance, a hidden manna, a divine grace, a something, call it what you will. I have something; I love It and I tabernacle with It. I do not mind if sometimes the outer picture is not all that it should be, because I know how many generations of material-mindedness there are behind me, and some of it must still be there. But I do have a hidden meat, a something, a wine, a water that the world knows not of. It is wholly spiritual, and I am willing to let It manifest in whatever way It will, do for me whatever It will, and lead me in any direction It will.

"My kingdom is not of this world. . . . My peace give I unto you, not as the world giveth. . . . I have meat the world knows not of." This all refers to the hidden kingdom, that hidden manna that is within us. When we know that God has incarnated in us as spiritual identity, we call It the child of God, the son of God, the only begotten of the Father, or God, any name we like, or we can invent a new name. The old names have all turned into clichés, so if somebody can bring forth a new name, let us have it, but my favorite terms for It is: "I have meat." I do not know what It is. I cannot describe It, but I have a something in me, and I know that It is living my life. I know that It puts these words in my mouth, because I do not study for them in advance, or make them up. I know that very often It sends words out of my mouth that I never even knew before they came out.

How can I convince you, not by these words but by the spirit of God that gives me these words, that you have a meat that the world knows not of? It is a substance capable of giving you the fullness of life. In God's presence, in the presence of this realized hidden manna, there is fullness of life. Do not ask how it will spring forth; do not ask how it is going to build a new lung for you; do not ask how it is going to build a new eye for you, if you need one. Drop all concern for this world, and realize that God did not send you into this earth and then cast you off to get along alone.

The God that is your Father and my Father is still your Father and my Father, and fortunately we do not have to search for His kingdom: He buried it inside us. All we have to do is to dig a little deeper into our own consciousness and unearth it. I have that divine presence within me that multiplies loaves and fishes. If my body is wrecked, It resurrects it, and in due time It will bring about my complete ascension above all material health and wealth, as well as poverty and sickness. Eventually we must be lifted up above health and wealth into the spiritual kingdom where the spiritual treasures are found.

Through our study of spiritual wisdom today we are laying up treasures "where neither moth nor rust doth corrupt."[17] What kind of treasures? This hidden manna, this hidden meat, the Word. There it is! It is the Word. "Man does not live by bread alone, but by every word that proceedeth out of the mouth of God." That word of God which is in the midst of us becomes flesh, appearing to us outwardly as health, harmony, wholeness, completeness, and perfection.

Crucifixion As an Internal Experience

If we can understand that every experience takes place within us, then we will know that whatever crucifixion we are called upon to endure is an internal crucifixion. It is crucifying the desires of the flesh. I do not mean that we should repress human nature or become ascetic and live on a crust of bread. If the Master increased loaves and fishes, surely it is meant that we are to have abundance, and even twelve basketsful left over to share. When I speak of crucifying the desires of the flesh, I mean crucifying the desire to pray for more things of the world, and rise higher in consciousness to a point where we are praying for the word of God, for a revelation of the hidden manna, the hidden meat, and the hidden kingdom.

We do not crucify anything in the external world. Leaving mother, father, brother, and sister does not mean abandoning our family. It means abandoning them inside in the sense of not being miserable if we do not see Mamma tomorrow. That is the kind of crucifying we have to do: to let Mamma live her own life and let us live our life, and yet love.

We crucify these human desires that make us parasites on other people or permit them to become parasites on us. Let us not have any of that. "I and my Father are one,"[18] and I must learn to live my life in God, with God. Then I can come out and tabernacle with you, share with you, and really have some of God's grace to give you. But the minute I begin living your life and letting you draw and pull on my personal life, I end up with nothing spiritual to give you. It is only as I learn to have my days, weeks, and hours alone with God that I have something for you when we do come together.

So it is with the members of our families. Every one of them has a right to his freedom, and each one must know that we have the right to ours, and then when we come together, we have something to give each other. Usually it is something of a spiritual nature made tangible in some form on earth.

"I have meat." It may not be in storehouses or barns. But it is certain that if I live long enough in the realization that I have this spiritual meat the world knows not of, I will also have full storehouses and barns. We cannot avoid ample supply when we are on the spiritual path; it has a way of gravitating to us. Probably for a very good reason it has been said that what we grasp and hold onto we lose; and what we loose we have. I think that is the explanation of it! So we release this human world and say to ourselves, "I am not thinking now in terms of entertainment; I am not thinking in terms of what I want to eat or wear: I am thinking now in terms of this 'meat that the world knows not of.' I am thinking in terms of this kingdom." The longer we dwell in that consciousness, the more material things there are to be enjoyed when we come back to earth.

Secrecy

The whole of the spiritual experience takes place within us. The crucifixion, the death, the resurrection, the ascension: all these take place within our consciousness, and we need not let the world know that it is going on. As a matter of fact, just as the parents of the Master took him down to Egypt and hid him for a few years, so it is far better to take our Christ and hide It within our own consciousness, not wearing our heart on the sleeve, not telling our neighbor what we are doing, and not trying to save him or his life until we have found our own. Far better to let the world alone for a little while until we have found our Christ and really have It to share. If we begin to share It too soon, we lose It, because we have not yet made It our own. We are not even certain of what we have.

Most of our students know that for sixteen years after my first spiritual experience I did healing work but I did no teaching until I knew what I had to teach. It took sixteen years to find that out and be absolutely certain that it was so. Because there was a certainty before I began to teach, it has lasted, prospered, and gone forth. When people tried to show me how wrong I was, they were unable to influence me, because I had been watching it for sixteen years and knew what it would do. I know what it is capable of, so I can teach it and even if all the world contradicts it, it cannot change one iota of what I have seen in these last thirty-odd years.

So it must be with you. If you are at the period of turning away from this world, do it silently, do it sacredly, do it secretly. If you are in the position of crucifying your human or corporeal desires, do not let the world know about it, because as far as the world is concerned, it is an insane project. Why? This is the only world human beings can see. Would it not be foolish to leave it? But once you have glimpsed the truth that this is not the only world, you will understand that it is not even a real world, but a world made up of bangles and baubles, of artificiality, hypocrisy, lies, false dealings, man's inhumanity to man, of physical and mental laws that cripple and defile. And yet we want a little more of it.

The Magnificence of the World
When Seen Through Spiritual Discernment

When we see the world face to face instead of "through a glass, darkly,"[19] the way the human mind sees it, this is the greatest world that ever could be imagined. This is really the world God created; this is really heaven right here on earth, but not the way the materialist sees it or the way the three-dimensional mind sees it. They are seeing "through a glass, darkly," and through the eyes of good and evil, they are seeing a distorted world. They are seeing good here and evil there, good today and evil tomorrow. Only when this fourth-dimensional consciousness or spiritual discernment has been developed, only then do we find that everybody in this world is just made up of love. All that is ever offered us is love, integrity, wisdom, joy, and sharing. It is a magnificent world when we are looking out through the eyes of God, with the vision of the Master, looking out and beholding the world of God's creating. We cannot see that with our eyes and we cannot hear it with our ears. It is the music that takes place within us the moment we begin to discern that which is invisible, when we begin to hear that which is inaudible and to see that which is incorporeal.

Then we understand the mystical language of "the meat" that the world knows not of and of living "not by might, nor by power, but by my spirit."[20] We might think that these scriptural terms are just stage settings or words in a play. They are not. They attest to reality. When the Master spoke of this meat, wine, and water, the bread of life, resurrection, the kingdom of God here and now, and of *My* grace, he was not being poetic. He was revealing an actual kingdom that exists on earth, but he knew that it would take something more than intellectual knowledge to become aware of it. In other words, we must not try to convince the people of this world of the hidden kingdom until they develop that inner eyesight. Then we can reveal it to them.

Most of you have been listening to this message and reading these writings for many years. By now you must have discerned that God's kingdom is here on earth, that it is available to us, that we have a hidden meat, a hidden manna, a whole new realm. It is within us that we discover this kingdom, but we discover it in proportion as we relinquish our desire and our prayers for corporeality.

Let us remember the words: *corporeal, corporeality, incorpo-reality.* Let our desires be for the incorporeal; let our prayers be for the hidden wisdom, the hidden glory, that it may be revealed. This will develop consciousness to the point of discernment where we, too, can sit beside the sick, close our eyes to the appearance, and then hear someone say, "I am better." It comes only through the development of inner discernment.

I caution students not to go into the healing work too soon. Even if they have learned all the words in my writings, they will not heal anybody of anything. If the words would heal, I would just beg, borrow, or steal money, if necessary, to have them printed and sent out into the world. I know better than that. I know that those words are not going to heal anybody. But if they are studied well, they will develop that inner discernment, that spiritual consciousness, and then the consciousness that has been developed will heal the sick.

It is not the books that do it; it is not the tape recordings of my classes that do it; it is not the classes: it is the consciousness that is built by means of the books, the tapes, and the classes. That is why all these adjuncts are helpful to us, not because they have any value in and of themselves. The value is in the consciousness they develop. Then we can travel the world without purse or scrip, because we have an inner meat, an inner wine, an inner water, an inner inspiration, guidance, direction, spiritual perception.

Glimpses into Past Lives and Future Experiences Possible

Life is a circle which includes pre-existence, life as we know it here, and the life that we will know as we leave here. The question is asked, "Are there those who know anything about their pre-existence, their life before they came here?" At a certain point in an individual's spiritual development, this capacity has developed to the extent that it is possible to see the past and the future as well as the present. It is not given to anyone to use as a vaudeville act: it is given to one only as a need may arise for a particular wisdom.

Those who have been shown their previous lives were not shown them just to satisfy a curiosity, but because it served a purpose in their present life. It gave them some light on why they are doing what they are doing, what is necessary to avoid previous mistakes, or what help could be given at this particular time in carrying on whatever the work might be, because those to whom it is revealed are often engaged in a spiritual activity.

With spiritual discernment, one is able to see into the human mind, and for that reason very often one not only can see past experiences in one's own life and in the lives of those around, but very often future experiences, things that have not yet come to pass. This, too, can be helpful, as long as it is kept wholly pure.

A man of my acquaintance had the ability to see into the human mind, and it became generally known among a number of people. One day a man came to him and, without mentioning his purpose, led my friend into conversation, and ultimately came to the question he had come to ask. "Well, who do you think is going to be elected President in this election?" My friend immediately saw, not only who was going to be elected, but by how much, and he mentioned it to this man, who later made quite a fortune through using that information. Unfortunately, my friend lost his prophetic vision for one whole year. One year later, on the very day that he had lost this capacity, it was returned to him, but by that time he knew how to be careful with the gift that had been given to him and not to throw his pearls before swine. This vision is not given to us for other men to gamble with. Many wonderful things become known as we rise in consciousness. We can see down into the human mind, and as long as that is for a useful purpose all is well.

The Circle of Life

Life is a circle. The day that we call our birthday is not the date of our real birth. This is the date in which we become visible on this plane. It does not mean that we were not visible on another plane a minute before, for we were; but now we become visible on this plane, and we will be visible on this plane for a part of that circle. Then we will go into invisibility, but we will still continue in that circle of life. We will probably come into visibility on another plane, and then we will go into invisibility again. So we will find ourselves in a complete circle of existence that never had a beginning and will never have an ending. It will result in birth and rebirth until such time as material consciousness has been completely overcome.

When we enter the state of spiritual consciousness that has no more of materiality in it, no more of good and evil in it, then we will find ourselves functioning totally on the spiritual level without returning to this schoolhouse of human existence. We are all learning lessons, and we are all being prepared for graduation into something higher and something better. Those who are on the spiritual path fulfill that function. Those who do not reach the spiritual path during this lifetime come back again on the material plane until such time as they do enter the spiritual path. From that moment on, they, too, are prepared for a spiritual destiny.

Chapter Five

The New Dispensation of Prayer

If long ago we had realized that the grace, power, and presence of God could come into our experience only through our soul-faculties, rather than through our mind, we would have understood, not only the nature of God but the nature of prayer. It is through prayer that God enters our individual and personal experience. When Paul told us that if we are carnally minded we are "not subject to the law of God, neither indeed can be,"[1] it should have awakened us to the truth that we cannot go on as human beings, praying to God, and then expect that the bounties, the joys, and the fruitage of God will come into our experience. God, Spirit, cannot be added to a material consciousness. For this reason, the Master made it clear that spiritual living and spiritual harmony can be brought into our experience only by dying to our human selfhood and being reborn into spiritual consciousness.

The New Teaching Cannot Be Added
to the Old Human Way of Life

First of all, Jesus made the necessity for rebirth clear when he taught, "Ye have heard that it hath been said, An eye for an eye, and a tooth for a tooth: But I say unto you, that ye resist not evil."[2] In those days it was right to punish, to judge, to condemn; it was all right merely to be obedient to the Ten Commandments; it was perfectly all right in those old days to treat others as they treated us. That was in the olden days, the days of the Hebrew period of unenlightenment and spiritual ignorance.

The Master, however, is carrying the people of his day over into a new dispensation. He is talking to the Hebrews, but not the Hebrews of the days of Abraham, Isaac, Jacob, and Moses: he is now talking to the Hebrews who have had a couple of thousand years during which, by means of obedience to the Ten Commandments, they should have been ready for a higher way of living. He brought this higher way of living to them, but he also told them in so many words that they could not add to a vessel already full; they could not take this new dispensation, this new teaching that he was about to give them, and add it to their old human way of living. They must "die daily"[3] to that; they must empty out their consciousness of materialism and be reborn.

Until we can accept the premise that we cannot go on being the same human beings we always were and simply add to that the grace of God, there is no way to enter the harmonies of spiritual living. It has been taught for many centuries that we must obey the Ten Commandments, not wholly, of course, because some say it would be too radical to expect a full obedience to them, but as nearly as possible we should obey the Ten Commandments. That, however, has not brought about harmony in individual relationships or in community or national relationships. Integrity in our government and in many facets of human experience has not yet been achieved. We are far from the day of demonstrating even the Ten Commandments in our community, national, and international life. We are far from living in obedience to good humanhood.

Why Discipline Is Necessary

The few who embark on the spiritual life find it difficult, and it is difficult. There is no question about that. Anyone who would try to make it appear that the spiritual life is easy to attain is misleading us. True, it is an easy life to live; it is a glorious, fruitful, abundant, and joyous life—but only after its attainment. The period of making the adjustment and of dying to the old self is not easy, and not always of short duration. The fact that living the spiritual life is not an easy way should not disturb us because, if we are determined to attain the spiritual way of life, we must be prepared for a period of struggle, effort, study, and discipline.

Why the discipline? We really have no struggle with morality, that is, we have not too great a struggle in this period in obeying the Ten Commandments. Most persons live for the most part in accordance with them. Why, then, the struggle? The main struggle for us is that we are the product of centuries of living exclusively in the external. Not only are there centuries of materialistic living behind us, but right in our cribs we began to live with rattles and dolls, later with marbles, and with every other kind of game that would keep our attention centered on the outer world. Sadly enough, even when we entered school more attention was usually paid to keeping us entertained and occupied with games and sports than with intensive study or with teaching us how to be still enough inside so that we could concentrate. Because of this preoccupation with nonessentials, there are only a few who have developed the ability to concentrate and who know how to study.

An ability to find an inner peace and stillness is required in following the spiritual path. Our entire demonstration rests on our attaining the ability to be so quiet in mind that we can hear the "still small voice"[4] and receive impressions from within.

The Cause of Much Failure in Prayer

Prayer has nothing to do with words that we think or speak. As a matter of fact, thoughts and words, except as a preliminary preparation, are barriers to the success of our prayers. Prayer is not something that goes from man to God. Prayer is that which flows from God to man, and the only time we are praying is when we are receiving, either hearing a message or feeling some inner impulsion or impression. When we are on the receiving end in quietness and in stillness, we are in prayer; but when we are thinking or speaking, we are not in prayer and nothing that we may think or state ever reaches God.

If this is true—and I am speaking after thirty years of experience—we can readily understand the failure to receive the benefits of prayer. This explains why peace has not come on earth or why peace has not even come to many individuals and also why God's government has not come to man. Man is not God-governed until he is able to receive from God. Man is never God-governed while he is thinking thoughts up to God, making speeches to God, reading prayers out of books, or reciting prayers from memory. None of this ever reaches God.

Words and Thoughts, a Preparation for Prayer

There is a place for words and thoughts in reaching God, but that place is a preparatory one. When we are about to pray, it is legitimate to engage in a form of what might be called contemplation or contemplative prayer. If, for example, we wish to pray and have had a busy day in the home or the office, we may not be able immediately to enter a deep enough silence to hear

that still small voice or to receive God's gift. We, therefore, prepare ourselves with a form of contemplative prayer in which we
may have many thoughts.

> I am entering prayer, not for the purpose of
> getting God to do something, but in order
> to bring myself into receptivity to God's grace.

> I am not entering prayer for the purpose of
> enlightening God. My heavenly Father knows
> my need, and it is His good pleasure to give me
> the Kingdom. Therefore, I am not trying to
> influence God or trying to bring God to me:
> I am going to mold myself so that I may receive
> the light which is already within me.
> The kingdom of God is within me and as
> I become still, I "open out a way for the
> imprisoned splendor to escape."[5]

> I am not asking God to destroy my enemies;
> I am not asking God to help me, to give me
> anything, or to do anything for me. I know
> that God knows enough to be God. I know
> that God has the power to be God-power,
> and I know that God's presence is
> already here where I am.

The purpose of my going into prayer is to be receptive, so
that I can hear, receive, commune with God, and be at-one with
the source of all life. These words and these thoughts have not
reached God or brought God into my experience, but they have
quieted me; they have settled me into an understanding of the
nature of prayer. It has been a reminder to me that I am not trying to use God for some purpose or make God my servant, but
that I am the child of God; I am the servant; I am the one to be

instructed, not God; I am the one to be enlightened, not God; I am the one who is to be influenced, not God.

The Listening Attitude of Prayer

The exact opposite of what we have been taught about prayer is the new dispensation of prayer, so that after this contemplative meditation, we are settled into an inner peace, and our inner ear is opened. We are in a receptive state of consciousness, listening and ready to receive whatever impartation the Spirit may have for us. Now the presence of God can come into our experience: the power of God, the joy, the life, and the wisdom of God can flow into us from within us. We must never forget that this God to whom we are praying to whom we are attuning ourselves, is within us. We are not thinking up to heaven; we are not thinking out into the world; we are attuned to the center of our own being from which the grace of God flows.

"Be still, and know that I in the midst of you am God."[6] Let each one of us, silently and sacredly, gently, within ourselves, breathe the word *I:*

> *I, I!* Be still, and know that *I* am God. *I, I* in the
> midst of you am mighty. *I,* the presence of God,
> the spirit of God, the life of God, the mind of God
> at the center of your being am speaking to you
> and *I* say to you: "Son, thou art ever with me,
> and all that I have is thine."[7] All that *I* at the
> center of your being has is yours.
>
> "I will never leave thee, nor forsake thee."[8]
> *I* will be with you unto the end of the world.
> *I* in the midst of you, the *I* that you voice secretly,
> sacredly, peacefully, that *I* in the midst of you
> is mighty. Be not afraid, for *I* will turn
> "to flight the armies of the aliens."[9]

Fear not the problems of this world: *I*, that *I* in the
midst of you, has "Overcome the world."
Fear not. Fear not! "I have overcome the world."[10]
I that is in the midst of you always will overcome
the world. Do not ask Me to do it. Be still, and
let there be light; let there be water, let there be the
earth; let there be crops; let there be fulfillment.
Just be still; be and let, for *I* in the midst of you
am the only might, the all-might; *I* go before you
to prepare a place for you; *I* go before you to
"make the crooked places straight."[11]
I go to prepare "mansions."[12]

"In quietness and in confidence shall be
your strength."[13] In quietness! "Not by might,
nor by power, but by my spirit"[14]—not by physical
doing, not by mental manipulation, but by
My Spirit, the spirit of God, that is in the
midst of you. Be still! Be still, and know that
I in the midst of you am God.

The moment the voice begins to speak to us, the earth
melts. We cannot hear the voice being uttered when we are talking, thinking, or striving. We can hear the voice being uttered
only when we are still, when we are in quietness, confidence,
and assurance. When we realize the nature of God in the midst
of us, then that voice can utter Itself, and the earth of problems
and errors will melt.

Living Out From a State of Receptivity

Authors, composers, inventors, and scientists all know what
it means to be still and let their literature, music, or inventions
flow from the depths of their withinness. If anyone doubts that
those things come from God, they are not aware of the nature

of God's activity in our experience. We can be in any activity of commerce, industry, housekeeping, or building, and find it true that "except the Lord build the house, they labor in vain that build it."[15] Were we a watchman, we would stay awake in vain, because "except the Lord keep the city, the watchman waketh but in vain."[15]

Unless there is a Grace, a Spirit, a Presence flowing through us out into our lives from deep down within, we are not yet at the spiritual level. We are at the spiritual level of living only when we can, at least in some measure, feel as Paul did when he said, "I live; yet not I, but Christ liveth in me"[16]; or the Master, "I can of mine own self do nothing.[17]. . . The Father that dwelleth in me, he doeth the works."[18]

Until we develop the ability to let that Spirit within live our life and let that Presence come forth in tangible form, we are not God-maintained or God-sustained. Instead, we are living by might and by power: by money, investments, securities, property, or by the sweat of our brow, not by the grace of God. The grace of God begins when we have attained a degree of inner stillness so that This that is within us may escape. It begins with the acknowledgment:

> The kingdom of God is within me.
> The name, the identity of God is *I*,
> the very Selfhood of me.
> I have no selfhood apart from God;
> I have no mind apart from God.
> Even my body is the temple of God.

With that realization, we find an inner stillness, and then the grace of God flows into active expression. While we continue about our daily work, we now discover that there are two of us: *I*, the inner Self which is greater than I, the outer self. In the Master's words, "I and my Father are one,"[19] but "my Father is greater than I."[20]

In reality we are one, not two, but we have an inner Self which is God and an outer self which is the son of God. The outer self and the inner Self are one, but the inner Self is greater than the outer self. When our conscious thinking is stilled, then our inner Self, the divine consciousness, the spirit of God, can speak, live, think, and act through us. We live; yet there is a Spirit within us that also lives. There is an indwelling Spirit that performs those things that are given us to do. It perfects that which concerns us, but It cannot come into our experience while we are thinking and talking or trying to persuade, influence, or bribe God.

Opening Ourselves to God's Guidance and Government

God will not respond when we tithe if our tithing has an ulterior motive. We cannot sacrifice, we cannot bribe, we cannot influence God in anyway. We can only be still! It makes no difference if we are in sin. Never for a moment does that stop the activity of God. On the contrary, that is more apt to bring it into expression. God has more pleasure in the lost sheep that is found than in the ninety-nine that were not lost. Part of the Master's mission was the forgiveness and healing of sin. Is it not usually some sin, disease, or lack that compels us to admit,"My way has not been sufficient. This human way of life has not done me much good." It is very much like the person who said to me, "I do not believe in God. Just look at my life and see if you could believe in God."

My response was, "You are proving definitely that you do not believe in God: you do not have a trace of God's influence in your life, do you?"

"No."

"So you do not believe in God. How, then, are you going to have God in your life? Do you expect God to knock you down and make you unconscious and then deliver His good to you when you cannot refuse it?"

We are closing ourselves to God, more or less, all the time, and then complaining that God is not doing anything for us. This is not our fault. It is because we have been taught to believe that prayer is something we do and that it consists of words and thoughts, whereas prayer is something we receive and consists of the ability to hear the still small voice. We do not instruct God: we let ourselves be instructed by God. We do not tell God: we let God tell us. The voice of God is mighty, but let It be uttered and expressed within us. Let It find outlet, and then we will dis-cover how God changes our nature. It is the difference between a life that we govern and a life that God governs. To be God-governed, the faculty of listening must be developed:

Instruct Me, Guide Me, Lead Me!

Often the spiritual life comes alive in us if we are familiar with some of the passages of scripture that reveal the nature of the spiritual life. Throughout all ages there have been spiritual masters, seers, saints, and prophets. These were not people who tried to talk to God or to get God to do their will. These were men, who developed the capacity to hear God.

In ancient days, for the most part, women were not permit-ted to partake of the spiritual life because by the time they had brought their children into the world, reared them, and taken care of the housekeeping, the farming, and some of the build-ing, they did not have much time left for spiritual things. Men had more time to contemplate, often contemplating what the women were doing at home. Sometimes it became so painful to see the women working so hard that they left home and went to the synagogue where they could rest in peace. So the men became the prophets. With changes in the social structure, how-ever, from now on, we can expect more from women. "God is no respecter of persons."[21] A child can listen and eventually hear and be instructed; anyone can: it is a matter of developing that faculty of stillness and quietness. All the scriptures of the world agree on this basic truth.

Dying to Human Consciousness

While we are dying to the old self and in the process of being reborn, we have access to the wisdom of those ancient wisemen, and we can learn from them how to prepare ourselves to receive. The Master gave us such instruction probably more clearly than anyone else has ever done. He was very bold and spoke plainly to his followers, so plainly that he was crucified for it. He told his followers what is necessary to enter this new dispensation: "Pray for them which despitefully use you, and persecute you. . . . For if ye love them which love you, what reward have ye?"[22] These words are not quoted very often, but they are certainly of equal importance to anything else that the Master said, and they bear out another passage of scripture in which he taught: "If thou bring thy gift to the altar, and there rememberest that thy brother hath ought against thee; leave there thy gift before the altar and go thy way; first be reconciled to thy brother, and then come and offer thy gift."[23] In other words, our prayers are not reaching the spiritual throne while we are entertaining thoughts of malice, enmity, or any other malpracticing thought.

In order to be a clear transparency through which God acts, we must remember that the nature of God is love and the more we can bring our own consciousness into an at-onement or attunement with love, the more receptive we will be to the voice of God. Therefore, we make a practice of remembering that man is spiritual. What far-reaching effects can such a realization have! Man is spiritual. That does not mean some men; it does not mean only good men, it does not mean only our allies. It means man. Man is spiritual. We cannot be at peace with our brother until we come into the realization that man is spiritual. It makes no difference whether we are thinking in terms of white or black, Jew or Gentile, ally or enemy, the truth is that man is spiritual.

Somehow each one of us must die to his hate, jealousy, animosity, bigotry, and prejudice. We cannot do this by wanting to do it; we cannot do it by wanting to change our thinking from wrong thinking to right thinking. We can do it in only two ways. First of all, it must be clear in our consciousness that there is only one God, a God closer to us than breathing. There is no man, woman, or child who has not the kingdom of God within him, whether in Europe, Asia, Africa, Australia, North or South America. Once we realize this, we cannot hate, envy, or fear anymore. We will never fear "man, whose breath is in his nostrils,"[24] if we have once seen that God is in the midst of him. We are not concerned now with whether he knows it or not: it is our knowing this truth that will make us free; it is our knowing this truth that will help to free this world.

One Selfhood

When we are convinced that there is but one God, that God in the midst of us is omnipresence, and that that God is the God of all mankind, we have taken the first step toward making peace with our brother, because now we have no enmity toward him. The second of the two great Commandments enjoins us to love our neighbor as our self. Humanly this is impossible because nobody can love every human being, and certainly not those who are guilty of some of the evils in which they indulge. From no human standpoint can we love our neighbor as our self.

But there is a way. The first part of that way is to know and to have only one God, and that God the God of all people. The second step is what makes it possible to fulfill the Master's command: "Thou shalt love thy neighbor as thyself."[25] This makes it possible to return to the altar to pray and to be assured of answered prayer. Since God is the one self-hood, the self of all being, the only self, the only life, the only soul, then my selfhood is your selfhood, his selfhood, or her selfhood. There is only one Self.

"Inasmuch as ye have done it unto one of the least of these my brethren, ye have done it unto me."[26] Why? Because just as *I* am the selfhood of the least of these my brethren, so am *I* the selfhood of all the others. Inasmuch as you have done it unto the other self, you have done it unto *Me,* for the self of him and of you is the self of *Me.* But "inasmuch as ye did it not to one of the least of these, ye did it not to me."[27] Why? What you do to another, you do to yourself, because there is only one Self. What you do not do for another is not being done for you because there is but one Self.

In that moment, then, we recognize that since God is the self, God is the life, soul, and spirit of every individual. Every selfhood is made up of the same life, the same soul, the same spirit, the same substance. The self of me is the self of you, and that which I do to you I do to my self. That which I do not do for you is not done for me. Beholding one God, one selfhood, and knowing my own human faults, how can I possibly hold you in bondage to your human faults? If I set myself free with the realization that God constitutes my being, how can I do less than set you free by knowing that God constitutes your being?

Temporarily you will be aware of my human errors, and I will be aware of yours, but the degree of our spiritual life is shown forth by our ability to look through the appearance and realize that God constitutes your selfhood and, therefore, I must do unto you as I would have you do unto me.

When I recognize that God constitutes your selfhood, I have made peace with you and am living harmoniously with you. As a matter of fact, you would very quickly find that you could not really be too angry with me or have a serious quarrel with me. You might not approve of everything I say or do, but you would be my friend. I would have made you my friend by knowing you as you really are, the son of God, the offspring of God, the selfhood of God. In this way I have established peace between us. One of these days we will establish peace on earth by realizing that God constitutes every living soul, and that the selfhood of one is the selfhood of all. Thereby we will take the enmity out of the consciousness of all peoples of the world.

The Basis of All Spiritual Living

"Inasmuch as ye did it not to one of the least of these, ye did it not to me." With this one lesson we have the basis of all spiritual living which is that I and the Father are one. But if we leave out any individual anywhere, we are losing our demonstration. We cannot say, "I and my Father are one," and then omit anyone else, without being an egotist. If we can agree that I and the Father are one, how wrong it would be to leave out a single individual of any race, creed, or national origin. If a thing is spiritually true, it means it is universally true, so if I and the Father are one, this is a universal truth. Let us bring the enemy into this circle of oneness with God, and see how much enmity can remain.

When I say, then, that the spiritual path is difficult, it is because it may be difficult at first to look around the world and as we recall a few names and faces, say with disbelief, "What? You, too, are one with God?" No, judging by appearances; but in truth I and the Father are one is a universal truth.

Declaring these statements of truth does not make them true. They were true in the beginning, but they have influence or power in our lives only in the degree of our acknowledgment of them. That solves the mystery of why God is not in the human picture, and yet why God can be brought into the human picture. God *is,* but God cannot function through material sense. God can function only spiritually, and there must be a spiritual ground or spiritual consciousness. In other words, consciousness must be purged of its humanness, of its twoness, of its duality, of its good and its evil, so that this presence which is within us can come forth.

In the degree, then, that we begin to behold God as one, God as spirit, God as universal, and God as individual selfhood, our consciousness is prepared to hear the voice and to feel that presence of God. If we work with such passages as, "Except the Lord build the house, they labor in vain that build it,"[28] or "He performeth the thing that is appointed for me,"[29] or "The Lord will perfect that which concerneth me,"[30] we cast fear out of ourselves. We cast out the belief that we alone are running our lives, and we thereby open ourselves to an inner conviction that there is a He.

Almost all of human experience is lived without an absolute conviction that there is a He. True, there is always a belief that there is a God, but I am talking about an actual inner conviction that there is a He, a He within me that is greater than I, a He within me that performs that which is given me to do. Even if we have gone far enough to agree on this, we may not have taken the second step. We may not have agreed that He is also within our enemy.

It profits us nothing to pray for our friends. We must know the truth about our enemies if we would be children of God. It is necessary that we agree that there is a He within him and her and it, as well as a He within us. We must agree that there is a He within the Jews, the Catholics, and the Orientals, as well as a He within the Protestants. Probably more especially we must agree that there is a He within everyone, as well as a He within the metaphysicians who are declaring It. The others may not be declaring It, but the same He is within them. They may not even be aware of It, but they have It, and our recognition of It brings It into expression in them. That is the secret of spiritual healing work.

God As Individual Being, a Universal Truth

Truth students may be ill, unemployed, or unhappy, and seek spiritual help. It seems strange that this should be, since those who are metaphysicians already know the truth about themselves, but that degree of conviction has not yet come, so they turn to a practitioner. The practitioner realizes the universal nature of God as individual being. The practitioner knows that the same truth that is true about him is true about every "you." What is true about one is true about all. The practitioner on the spiritual path never gives or addresses a treatment to a patient. He never prays for a patient. The practitioner on the spiritual path knows the truth, a universal truth, because if it is true about him, it has to be universally true, or God is not one and God is not omnipresence.

Until we open ourselves to the realization of God as absolute, universal being, and of God as constituting individual being, we are not praying. When we realize this and pray the universal truth, then we are opening the consciousness of everyone to the truth about themselves.

This principle works in a miraculous fashion for us when we begin to perceive that God constitutes the being of every individual who comes within range of our experience. We are called upon, therefore, to spend more time knowing the truth about those we do not like and those who do not like us than we spend knowing the truth about our friends. A little meditation for our friends will do, but it requires a great deal of meditation for those who are not our friends, before we come into the realization of this oneness that exists among all of us.

ACROSS THE DESK

We are confronted on every hand with the words *energy crisis:* This universal problem must be met, not on the level of the problem, but through the active practice of specific spiritual principles. And what really is energy? Energy has its basis in a purely spiritual source, independent of waning fossil fuel, natural gas, nuclear power, or any of the other known and visible sources of fuel. Energy is the impetus of a divine activity of consciousness which fulfills Itself as us. It is inherent in all being, an integral part of being, and we are not separate from the infinite outpouring of the energy of Spirit.

New energy sources can easily and quickly open up as we perceive the nature of energy as infinite Spirit ever present. The world mesmerism that human greed, self-interest, international economics and politics govern the supply of energy must be broken. This can be done only by the conscious realization that Spirit is omnipresent and, therefore, energy as an activity of Spirit is omnipresent and infinite, manifesting and sustaining itself effortlessly without barrier or obstacle.

Students of the Infinite Way should work daily on this immediate problem by being the transparencies for spiritual energy, ever active in consciousness, to pour out to the world.

Chapter Six

Demands of the Spiritual Life

To die to our human selfhood and to be reborn is something which is consciously attained. It is a conscious act. To help us attain that state, the Master gave us a formula, which no one has ever improved upon: "Ye shall know the truth, and the truth shall make you free."[1] Part of what constitutes the difficult process of dying and being reborn is that inwardly we resent or resist knowing the truth. We would much prefer to take it for granted that since God is love, we have only to leave it to God and all the rest will be done for us. But it is not that way.

The act of dying and of being reborn is accomplished through a conscious knowing of the truth; it is a praying without ceasing.[2] It is not something we can do for five minutes a day, or even for an hour, and then feel that all of God's grace is flowing through us. Actually, it is a constant knowing of the truth with every situation that arises in our experience, and this may last for many years.

Beginning the Day With an Acknowledgment of God

Ordinarily we awaken in the morning and, sooner or later, jump out of bed, make our physical preparations for the day, have breakfast, and then go off about our business. Such a program does not make possible a dying to our humanhood. In order to bring to an end the changing good and evil experiences of our lives, which constitute humanhood, we have to embrace truth *consciously* each day as we awaken.

On awakening, the realization might come that day has followed night. We did not have to sit up and watch it; we did not have to pray about it or take thought about it. In fact, there is no record of any time when day did not follow night, or night follow day, so there must be some law in operation. It is a law that neither you nor I can control; it is a law that operates without any help from us. So on awakening in the morning we are consciously aware that there is a law at work, something greater than we are. We might also feel a little sense of gratitude that the coming of day is not dependent on our remaining awake at night or even on our ability to pray, but that there is a law and a wisdom governing this earth.

Using Mealtime To Acknowledge the Source

When we come to breakfast, as a rule we either take for granted the food on our table, or perfunctorily give thanks to God for it, neither of which is quite correct. "In all thy ways acknowledge him, and he shall direct thy paths."[3] The breakfast table is an opportunity for an acknowledgment that "the earth is the Lord's, and the fulness thereof,"[4] that there is a law of God that keeps the earth filled with crops, fruits, and all the things necessary to our experience. Also it is an opportunity to know the truth for our neighbor—friendly neighbor or enemy neighbor—that since "the earth is the Lord's, and the fulness thereof," God's bounty fills the earth.

There is, of course, an appearance to the contrary. It would seem, in the human picture, that there is a tremendous scarcity of food in India, China, and Russia; but in reality there is as much potentiality for raising crops in those countries as there is in the United States and Canada. It may not be visible or tangible to those people because at the present time, they do not have the know-how to bring it forth. But they could know all that is to be known about agriculture, and that might not solve the problem, nor would money, because in many cases they have chosen to spend their resources on armaments rather than on food and consumer's goods.

The United States Is
Founded on Trust in God

When this country was founded, it was based more on a religious conviction than on guns. The founders of our country were very short on guns in the early days of this nation but long on religion, and it was the custom then to acknowledge God. Even the currency of the land, with its "In God we trust," is an acknowledgment of God. They had to place their trust in God, because they had not much of anything else. The demonstration of this entire nation has been a spiritual demonstration, resting on spiritual values. All the other things, all the other benefits that we have received, have been added unto us, because there has been in the consciousness of the nation a religious fervor from the very beginning. This does not exist in too many other countries. Religion is for the most part more formalized, and in many countries it is something quite separate and apart from the human scene, even though in some countries there is a state church, and the separation of church and state is not as clearly defined as it is in the United States.

Our founding fathers, however, did not think it unseemly to provide a day of thanksgiving in which to thank God even for the food in the ground, thereby connecting God with the very things of earth and not separating them from the grace of God. They did not believe that they got their food by the sweat of their brow alone or by finding favor with the Indians: they acknowledged God as the source of all good.

God is Not Separate and
Apart From Our Daily Experience

For centuries the church has held to the idea that God and health were two separate things. Health was something the doctors took care of, and evidently death was something God took care of. Health was never thought of as having anything to do with God. God and health were separated, and it is only in this past century that the spiritual ministry of Christ Jesus is being restored to the churches of most denominations, because once more it is being recognized that God cannot be separated from health.

If we acknowledge at our breakfast table that God is responsible for our daily food, for the crops in the ground and on the trees, it will be much easier when we leave home to see a connection between God and driving on the road, between our business or our profession. We will find it much easier to recognize that God should not be separated from our daily experience, but rather that God must be united with our daily experience. "Except the Lord build the house, they labor in vain that build it."[5]

God has been considered as something separate and apart from this world. That explains why there have been so few answered prayers. There has been no answer to the prayers for peace or prosperity on earth. It is not that God actually is separated from our breakfast, lunch, or dinner table; it is not that God actually is separated from peace on earth; it is that we have brought about a sense of separation by not acknowledging Him in all our ways. We have looked to temporal powers, depended on our bombs and battleships to bring us peace, instead of recognizing that even though temporarily there may be a necessity for all these arms and ammunition, there can be no peace without its being rooted and grounded in God. God must be an integral part of our daily life; God must be the central core of peace on earth. This is the crux of it. It must be done consistently, and it can be done only by a conscious act of Consciousness, consciously connecting God with our daily life. "The earth is the Lord's, and the fulness thereof," and in His presence here on earth where we stand is fulfillment.

When we consciously make contact with God, we have that fulfillment. When we consciously acknowledge God in all our ways, we have a greater sense of peace and well-being. When we consciously acknowledge that He that is within us is greater than he that is in the world, it becomes so to us. When we consciously acknowledge that He performs that which is given us to do, so it becomes unto us. Otherwise we have God in heaven and a life here, but by a conscious act of Consciousness, we can bring the two together.

The Individuality of Spiritual Identity

In the human picture an Infinite Way class might appear to be made up of a hundred people sitting out there in a room, and, as the teacher, I appear to be but one up here. If I accept this picture we can be friends, we can be enemies, we can be indifferent, or we can be a mixture of all of these. But I could stop all that nonsense in a very brief time. Within one week we can all be friends, and good lifelong ones too. This has nothing to do with human favoritism: it has to do with a conscious act of Consciousness. I must embody God in my consciousness and realize that the same God is embodied in your consciousness. I must recognize the same divinity in you that I have already discovered to be hidden somewhere in me. Then there is no possibility of enmity or disagreement. We all have opinions; we do not want to become IBM machines and all give the same answer.

As a matter of fact, it is on the basis of individuality that no one has to be a major prophet to see that communism is doomed. Why must this inevitably be? The reason is that God is individual consciousness, your consciousness and mine, and we are individual beings, each with an individuality. God is the oneness that flows through us, but it flows through us in individual ways, so that some of us are writers, some composers, some doctors, and some ministers. Each one is showing forth God in an individual way. We are not showing forth our own glory. Every bit of good that flows through us, even if it is only sending a check to the community fund, is the showing forth of God's love for our fellow man. Whatever we do in life glorifies God, but each one glorifies God in an individual way.

There are fathers and there are mothers; there are brothers and sisters; there are friends; and there are businessmen and artists. Each one of us in an individual way is an offspring of God, showing forth some facet of God. The more we acknowledge this, the better we are at our particular work. The more we believe that a talent is ours or the more we believe that we do not have a God-talent, the more we cheat ourselves.

A Conscious Act of Consciousness

The more we acknowledge that the very breath we breathe is God, the very life we live is God, and the very thoughts we think emanate from God, the more we will show forth God's glory. The more we abide in the truth of our spiritual identity and spiritual individuality, the more we bring forth of God, and the more harmonious, the more prosperous and the more complete we become.

Communism is a denial of this and negates individuality. It denies God-being and God-given talents. Every person becomes a slave of the state, because the state takes the place of God and exercises complete power and control over every individual. How much greater strength, youth, and talent is exhibited by those in the metaphysical and spiritual world who acknowledge God as constituting their being! How much greater success and peace follow those who attune themselves to God! And what must inevitably happen in the denial of individuality and the denial of individual integrity and capacity? Anything that plays down or negates man's individuality and his God-given capacities must in the end destroy him. As human beings rarely do we reach our full potentiality until the day when we admit that new component into our being: Spirit, the life and wisdom of the Father.

The moment we begin to admit the Presence consciously into our lives, we lose years from our appearance and we gain a sense of eternity and immortality. We cannot do it, however, merely by reading books or by hearing lectures. We do it only by a conscious activity of Consciousness. From the minute we awaken in the morning, we have to embrace God in our consciousness. In everything we do in every way we do it, we have to acknowledge that we are showing forth God's glory. Everything we do attests to God's presence and power in us. The more we acknowledge It consciously, the more we bring It into actual experience.

Loving God

In order to be alive, a mind has to think something. It will not do just to do right thinking: it has to be spiritual thinking, embracing the spirit of God and bringing It into individual expression.

What God is to us, God is because of our opening our consciousness to God. What God is not to us is in the degree of our closing our mind and our consciousness to God. Praying without ceasing is not just religious namby-pamby! Praying without ceasing means steadfastly keeping our mind, heart, and soul alive and alert in God. I do not think the master was being sanctimonious when he said, "Thou shalt love the Lord thy God with all thy heart, and with all thy soul, and with all thy mind."[6] In that statement, he gave us a law of life. We cannot love God mildly, nor can we love God by taking Him for granted. I admit that we do not have to make speeches about it and that it does not help to go around saying, "O God, I love You. O God, I love You with all my heart and with all my soul." As a matter of fact, I would certainly be suspicious of myself if I caught myself doing that, or of anyone else for that matter.

We love the Lord with all our heart and with all our soul in the degree that we take God consciously into our being, our business, and our body. This is loving God: knowing that God is fulfilling Himself in our individual experience, knowing that God is manifesting His eternal Life as us and through us, and that God is expressing His wisdom and His love through us.

Living Is Made Manifest in Activity, Not Idleness

Right from the beginning of my spiritual teaching ministry, the point has been emphasized that only in consciously embracing God do we have God; only in consciously embodying and acknowledging God do we have God. When the Master said, "I am the bread of life,"[7] he was asking us consciously to acknowledge that our bread is at the center of our being. It does not have to come to us. We do not earn it by the sweat of our brow. True, we work hard, but that is part of fulfilling one's self on earth.

The person who is not working hard is not truly living. Living is shown forth in the intensity of the work we are doing and the intensity of the joy that we find in doing it. Living is not made manifest in idleness or in doing nothing. Living is made manifest in an activity that we can love and enjoy. Such an activity will bear fruit, but only in proportion as consciousness is opened and we consciously see that God fulfills Himself as us, or He is not being fulfilled at all.

God Is Fulfilling Himself As Man

If there were no people on earth, the only way that God would be evident would be as trees, plants, or animals. But God does not come to fulfillment until He comes to fulfillment as man. A mortal being is not man; a person living separate and apart from God is not man; a person living an animal life on earth is not man; and a person hiding in bomb shelters is not man, either. We cannot find man there. These are little, scared animals, people afraid to live and afraid to die. If we are not afraid to live, we will not be afraid to die. At sometime or other we are all going to pass from this scene, but it will be a movement from glory to glory, unless we choose to go out like a pack of cowards. Let us stand up, and when we go out, go out like men and women, facing God, not trying to hide from temporal powers.

No man can ever die while he is alive in God. The only death that can come is to the animal man, and he can prevent it by giving up his animal nature and embracing God, if only he can learn about it in time.

There is no way for God fully to glorify Himself except as man. Otherwise there are masses of useless trees, useless gold, silver, diamonds, and pearls. God does not come to full glory until He comes to glory as man. And who is that man except the one who can acknowledge God? To be the fulfillment of God, man must understand that God is glorifying Himself through your individual frame and mine, and through his and hers. God is glorifying Himself and showing Himself forth in infinite form and variety, not as a lot of desolate and deprived slaves, not even as a lot of rich slaves.

The Freedom of Spiritual Man

Countries that do not have much of God have little real freedom. Where there is God there is freedom, for God is the only freedom there is. There is no real freedom except spiritual freedom. When we are spiritually free, we can understand why Paul could say, "Neither death, nor life. . . shall be able to separate us from the love of God."[8] Neither life nor death! That is a free man: free to live; free to die, if it is necessary, without whimpering, because he is free. He knows that wherever he moves he carries freedom with him, if he carries the spirit of God. Everyone has the spirit of God, but if he is not acknowledging It, he is not only unaware of Its presence, but he is not relying or depending on It. In other words, he has cut himself off from It, and the spirit of God is then of no avail.

There would be Eden on the face of the earth today if only we could acknowledge God in all our ways, if only we could acknowledge God fulfilling Himself as man, even fulfilling Himself as the dictators of the world. That acknowledgment might help to wake them up to their God-identity and change their idea that man is merely a servant of the state.

God Cannot Be Used

In bringing harmony into our experience and realizing that it must be consciously done, I would like to point out a particular principle that makes for the greatest degree of harmony and freedom in our experience if we will but consciously embrace it. This principle cannot be taken for granted, nor can a person say, "Oh, I know that." It makes no difference whether he knows it or not: what makes the difference is whether or not he practices it, and practices it over and over again, day after day. In this regard we would do well to remember Paderewski's statement that if he did not practice the piano one day, he knew it; if he did not practice two days, his manager knew it; and if he did not practice three days, the public knew it. If we do not practice this particular principle one day, we will know it; if we do not practice it a few days, our whole experience will show forth the lack of practice.

Religions have been built on the false premise that there is a great power and that if in some way we can earn, deserve, or get hold of It, It will destroy the discords in our life, remove our enemies, and heal our diseases. It is on this point that religion fails. There is no God that overcomes sin, disease, or death. There is no God that can be used as a great power. There is the key word: *used!* There is no God that can be used. The very first step in our discipleship is to realize the truth that God cannot be used.

When we settle down into prayer, let that be one of our very first thoughts: since God cannot be used, I am not here to use God. For a while, if we practice this faithfully, we will find it difficult. There will be the temptation to turn back and say, "O God, do this. O God, help me; O God, O God." But with every breath we have to turn away from such ideas:

> No, do not listen, God; do not listen to my pleas.
> I do not want to use You. I do not want to call on
> You for anything. I want to acknowledge that You are
> closer to me "than breathing, and nearer than hands
> and feet." I do not want You to do anything to any
> evil powers; I want to acknowledge that
> You are almighty, the only power.
>
> I will not fear what mortal man or mortal
> conditions can do to me. I will not fear what
> "the armies of the aliens"[9] can do to me;
> I will not acknowledge that they have any power.
> I will be like the Master, at least in a degree,
> and say, "Pilate—whether my particular
> Pilate happens to be a disease or a dictator—
> 'Thou couldest have no power at all against me,
> except it were given thee from above.'[10]
> Pilate, thou couldest have no power over me,
> for there is only one power, and it is
> God, Spirit, Life. I do not have to get It, earn It,
> deserve It, or pray for It: I have to acknowledge It."
>
> Let me not be tempted to turn to You for something.
> Just let me rest in the assurance of

Your presence, You fulfilling Yourself, You living
my life. I live; yet not I: You live my life. I live; yet
not I, but You live my whole experience.

Resist the Temptation to Turn to God

The biggest factor in spiritual healing is to resist the temptation to turn to God to bring about a healing. Instead we must acknowledge that God, Spirit, alone is the cause, the law, and the substance of all form, and that regardless of any appearance to the contrary, we will stand on this truth: "Judge not according to the appearance."[11] Appearances may testify to a sin or a disease; appearances may testify to something or other not of God, but if we judge by appearances, we are going to be a slave to appearances. To be free means to acknowledge that all that God made is good, and anything that does not conform to that standard is not God-ordained and has no law of God to enforce it.

To discipline ourselves not to turn to God expecting God to do something for us, is itself an indication of the difficulty of embracing the spiritual life, because the very idea of expecting God to do something for us suggests the idea that God is not doing it for us now. That is a denial of the truth that God is the same yesterday, today, and forever. It is a denial of omnipotence, omnipresence, and omniscience. To believe for a minute that God can do something for us after we have given a treatment or been given a treatment is a denial of God. The treatment should consist of the understanding of omnipresence, even before we pray.

God Is

"Before they call, I will answer."[12] *Before* they call! If we believe that God is going to operate after we have prayed, we have misunderstood the nature of God and have cut ourselves off from God. God is not going to act in the future. In God there is no time: no past, no present, and no future. There is only *now*. Now is the only time God is, and all that God is, God is now. All that God is ever going to be, God is being now; all that God ever was, God is now. All that God was in Galilee two thousand years ago, God is here and now this minute. All that God did in the Holy Land two thousand years ago through Jesus Christ, God is doing at this very moment, in this room, through us. Just as "God is no respecter of persons,"[13] God is no respecter of time. God did not pick two thousand years ago as the time to do healing work and leave all the people before that and all the people who have lived since then out in the cold. There is no such God.

Everything is an activity of consciousness and, therefore, we consciously, sometimes even unconsciously, cut ourselves off from God by accepting the opinions of the world. But we can stop that nonsense any time we choose and realize:

> What God was, God is, and what God is, God ever
> will be. God is omnipresence; God is omnipotence;
> and God is omniscience. God *is*, and that is enough.
> God is here and now where I am. "The place
> whereon thou standest is holy ground."[14]
> Here where I am is holy ground, for I and the
> Father are one. There is no separation between
> God and man! God shows Himself forth as man.
> God shows forth His whole glory as man, and that
> man is here and now, the man I am.

We open our consciousness to this truth and, as we embrace it, we embrace the whole of the Godhead. If we do not open ourselves to the truth, we are closing our consciousness to God, but that does not prevent somebody else's embracing it. "A thousand shall fall at thy side, and ten thousand at thy right hand; but it shall not come nigh thee,"[15] if we open our consciousness to the truth of omnipresence.

We Must Know the Truth

Is it not clear why following the spiritual path is difficult? It is difficult because the very simplicity of the principles makes us think that they do not have to be practiced. We do not awaken in the morning and consciously embrace God in our day. We do not go through the routine of realizing that God is responsible for all that is in the earth. "The earth is the Lord's, and the fulness thereof": the cattle on a thousand hills, the crops in the ground, the fruit on the trees.

Everything is God's, and whatever is God's is yours and mine. "Son, thou art ever with me, and all that I have is thine,"[16] but we must consciously embrace that truth in order to manifest it. The fact that it is the truth will not help us. "Ye shall know the truth"; then the truth we know will help us. But if we are not consciously embracing God, the activity of God, the substance of God, the law of God, the life of God, and the mind of God, we are not experiencing it.

It is like having money in the bank that we do not know about. As far as we are concerned, it is of no use to us. It is the same with God. We have all the God that anybody else has, even as much as Jesus Christ had. The difference is that Jesus Christ knew God so thoroughly that he lived with Spirit morning, noon, and night. He went away for forty days occasionally to contemplate It, meditate upon It, glory in It, rest in It, relax in It, and to let that Spirit so fill him that wherever he went, he was a benediction. Even his clothes were filled with the spirit of God, so that when a person touched his clothing he was healed. Why? There was no more of God in him than there is in us, but he was more consciously aware of It.

The whole secret is consciousness. Consciousness! Be conscious, know the truth: *I* will never leave you, nor forsake you. *I* will be with you to the end of the world. Know this truth; be conscious of it; live with it morning, noon, and night; pray without ceasing, and you will bring it into your experience.

The hypnotism of this world is so great, operating through subliminal perception however, that we are all receivers of the world's sadness and badness, and if we do not consciously separate ourselves from it and bring ourselves consciously into our oneness with God, we do not experience it and we do not enjoy it. If we get mentally lazy and just decide to read a book about it, we will lose it. The sad part is that we can have a lot of it today and lose it next year.

Reading the thirty odd books recounting my experiences on the path will not help anyone very much. Sometimes someone gets a healing through them; someone receives an uplift, someone enjoys some benefit. Many people read spiritual literature and have beautiful healings, but those are temporary things; they are not to be gloried in. The benefit that students can get from my thirty years is not in reading my books or hearing my tape recordings but in taking these principles of life and embodying them in their consciousness.

If I had not had to do the same thing, I would not tell students to do it. I have to keep it up as much as anyone else. I have to live morning, noon, and night in the conscious remembrance of these truths. I cannot let days go by, not even one day, not even an hour go by, without an activity of truth in my consciousness. I cannot answer my mail without turning, with every few letters, to that Spirit within for more light, more spirit, more and deeper awareness. And I know that no one else can either.

That is why I sing the same song always of consciously knowing the truth, of consciously opening ourselves to the presence of God, consciously letting God abide in us, consciously making God a part of our life and, never under any circumstances, trying to make of God a servant. Let us never try to get

God to do something for us, but open ourselves and *let* the spirit of God flow through us. It will do more than we can ask for. By contemplating the truth of God, by keeping the mind stayed on God, by pondering this idea of the Spirit as the All and Only, the mind settles into a beautiful peace that enables us to be receptive to the presence. "Thou wilt keep him in perfect peace, whose mind is stayed on thee."[17]

Across The Desk

Infinite Way students who have a real understanding of the principles of spiritual living do not go out with unrestrained evangelical zeal seeking to draw others to their particular path, teaching, or chosen teacher. In their zeal they may believe that they are doing God's work, but nothing could be further from the truth. Infinite Way students should know that God's work is already done and does not need any prodding for Its fulfillment. Proselytizing is no part of the Infinite Way activity.

Instead of thinking that he knows what someone else needs, the wise student will perform the greatest service to his fellow man by realizing the self-completeness of every individual and by trusting the consciousness of every person to fulfill itself. His realization of this truth in the silence of his own being will help to awaken those he longs to bring to a spiritual way of life far more effectively than meddling in the human scene or interfering in another person's life. Joel has said it very well in *A Parenthesis in Eternity,* pages 308-310:

> It is so easy to think that we can be of benefit to one another. This is the natural belief of the natural man, ego-man. One branch cannot really benefit another branch, however, because whatever benefit may come to you or to me through each other is really only the Life Itself using us as Its instrument. The blessings that come into our experience from any direction are really God Itself flowing to us. It is true, of course, that as servants of

the most High we also serve each other, but we serve only as instruments of God.

The truth that enables us to serve each other is knowing that I have nothing of my own to give you, and you have nothing of your own to give me: we derive our good from the same Source because we are one—one Tree. We are the manifestation of one Tree of Life and, by an invisible bond, we are all branches of that one Tree.

In living this life the mystic becomes a blessing without consciously desiring or attempting to be. All those who come into his presence feel something emanating from his consciousness. And what is it that they feel? Not any desire to do good: just the ability to live at the center in this contemplation of oneness.

There is no place for "do-gooders" or meddlers in the Infinite Way. Let the consciousness of every person, which in reality is God-consciousness, lead him to spiritual fulfillment, even though it may be by a way that he has no knowledge of at his present stage of unfoldment. Implicit trust in the Infinite Invisible and the realization that underneath this realm of appearances is a divine activity in operation are the mark of a true Infinite Way student.

Chapter Seven

Consciously Knowing
the Truth

The principle of one power is perhaps the oldest spiritual principle ever revealed. One of the first spiritual revelators of the principle of one power, if not the first, was Gautama the Buddha, who revealed that this world and the powers of this world—sin, disease, death, and poverty—are illusion, and that the only reality is spirit, the invisible, which alone is power.

On that basis, one of the first healing movements developed, a movement which spread throughout all India and eventually reached much of the rest of Asia. In its first few hundred years it is reported that marvelous healing work on a broad scale took place. The reason for this phenomenal success was that Gautama taught his followers that all evil is illusion, and they therefore should not fight evil, try to overcome it, or get rid of it.

The followers of Gautama, including some of his immediate disciples, however, did not have sufficient spiritual vision to understand the meaning of one power, so they set up *maya*, which means illusion, as a separate power and tried to have the first great power do something to the illusion. In so doing, the basic principle of Gautama's teaching was lost, and they failed. Whenever another power is set up, about which God is expected to do something, there is duality and there is no longer the possibility of healing.

Christ Jesus also established his healing mission on the principle of one power. To the man sick with the palsy, he said, "Arise, take up thy bed, and go unto thine house,"[1] which certainly indicates quite clearly that Jesus gave no power to that condition.

In one case Jesus applied spittle to a blind man's eyes[2] and healed him. Surely he was not implying that spittle was the healing agency for blindness, but rather that spittle, a substance which in and of itself is nothing, was enough to heal blindness. Why? Because blindness has no power to maintain itself, except in the minds of those who are under the influence of two powers.

So it is that even at the tomb of Lazarus, Jesus said, "Lazarus, come forth."[3] What he was saying was that there is no power in death. The only power death has is the power given it by accepting a belief in two powers. If life were understood as the only power, the thought of death would never enter the mind.

An Illusion Is Always in the Mind

The followers of Buddha gradually came to make the mistake of believing that *maya,* or the illusion, was out here. They began to be indifferent to the world as we know it, because if it is only *maya,* why bother about the world? The attitude developed that there is no use or point in trying to heal the body. Even today many followers of Oriental teachings do not permit themselves to be healed because they believe that the body is only an illusion which they are going to get rid of someday anyway, so why bother with it?

Laboring under their perception of the world as illusion, they became indifferent to progress. To them this world was illusion, *maya.* Why bother about it? Why build it up? In this

assumption they were mistaken. An illusion cannot be objecti-
fied. An illusion is an erroneous mental image in thought, never
outside of thought. When you see the illusion or mirage on the
desert, it is not outside. It is in your false perception of what you
are seeing. Even though you see the horizon in the distance,
there is no horizon out there. That is an optical illusion which
is within you. All you need to prove it is to keep going up and
up in a plane and watch the horizon recede. If you could go up
far enough, you would see the entire hemisphere, because the
horizon does not exist as externalized form; the horizon is a
mental percept within us.

There is a very interesting story from India about a man
who stepped into a rowboat on the river. When he did that, it
was now and here for him. Then he rowed a mile downstream,
and when he got there, the place he left was the past. It was far
away, and the place where he was then was here and now.
Ahead of him was the future, but it was over there. Yet when
he arrived there, he found it also was *here* and *now.* And so it
is that if you could go a little bit above the earth you would
find that what is called the past, the present, and the future are
all the present.

People Began to Fear the Illusion

Maya, or illusion, is a misperception of what you are
beholding, and to recognize that truth would make you an
instrument for healing. Not only that, it would save you from
the disastrous effects of the universal belief in two powers. The
moment that you take material or mental power and embrace it
in some term such as *illusion* or *carnal mind,* you can dismiss it,
knowing that what you mean by that is nothingness, the "arm
of flesh" of Hezekiah: "With him is an arm of flesh,"[4] temporal
power, nothingness. You have the one and only power there is:
God Almighty. When you have God Almighty, there is no other
power, and you are free.

After learning about the carnal mind, Paul had two powers also, making the carnal mind "enmity against God."[5] And what did it do to him? Every week he ended up in a prison or was beaten with stripes, and eventually he died there. He made a devil for himself and then set out to attack it. Since he created it and would not destroy it, he gave it life eternal and gave it more power than he gave himself.

The Principle of One Power

If you understand the principle of one power, you will perceive that there is no power external to you, either for good or evil. You will then not look for good to come to you even from God, and certainly you will never expect or experience any evil from a devil, Satan, carnal mind, or *maya*. Why? "The kingdom of God is within you."[6] That is a simple statement of an absolute truth. It means that the kingdom of power is within *you*. And since there is only one power, you do not even need to use it.

You can use material power and you can use mental power, but no one has ever been able to use spiritual power. Why? There is nothing on which to use it. There is nothing against which to use it. There is no opposite or opposition to God. There are no pairs of opposites. God is one: one power, one life, one consciousness, one soul, one being, one body. God is one, but since God is infinite, there is no other than that One, and that One is within you. You need only rest; you need only relax; you need only know this truth:

> The kingdom of God is within me. "Is there a God beside me? . . . I know not any."[7] Are there any powers other than the power that is within me? I know not any. Is there any other cause? I know not any. That *I* in the midst of me will never leave me or forsake me, and in It all power is embodied.

As long as you can say the word *I,* understanding the depth of meaning of that word, you are all right. You have infinite God-power and nothing else: nothing to overcome, nothing to destroy, nothing from which to protect yourself.

Are You Receptive to World Beliefs or to the Spiritual Impulse?

This brings the student to one of the most important aspects of Infinite Way teaching, found in the chapter "Protective Work," in *The Infinite Way Letters, 1955,*[8] and also in "Across the Desk," in *Our Spiritual Resources.*[9] If this work is understood, most of your other study becomes unnecessary. Everything that happens to you must happen through your own consciousness. What does not happen through your consciousness is never known to you. Therefore it is up to you to determine what will happen to you.

Unless you understand the principle involved, going through the motions will do you no good. The principle is that the mind is like an antenna, picking up everything that is in the air. This became obvious with the first experiments using subliminal perception in advertising. Advertising put out on the air waves, which could neither be seen nor heard, was obeyed.

Other experiments carried on by television induced people to get up from their seats and go to the telephone, only to find that they had no one to call and that no one had called them. They did not know why they had gone to the telephone. But because "Go to the telephone" was flashed on the air so quickly that they could neither see nor hear it, up they jumped and went to the telephone, and then wondered why.

So it is that in the morning, sometimes before you are out of bed and have an opportunity to read the newspapers, hear the radio, or watch television, you find yourself with a cold, and you wonder where it came from.[10] Later you learn from the radio, television, or newspaper that the country is in the throes of a flu epidemic, and that is the reason. But before you knew about it, you had responded to it.

You Protect Yourself, Not From a Power but From a Belief

Human beings are always obeying impulses from what is called this world, the universal mind, and not understanding why. You may wake up some morning feeling a terrible sense of fear. Then when you get up, you hear some bit of international news that makes you wonder what is going to happen next! But you knew it before you got out of bed; you already had the fear; and then you got up and found out why.

The human mind is forever picking up suggestions to which you and I respond and which act upon us physically, mentally, morally, or financially. It has been said that if a doctor in the other part of the world makes a discovery of a new disease today, by tomorrow there can be thousands of cases of that disease all over the world. You may wonder how the news could travel so fast. It didn't. It traveled silently, invisibly and hypnotically.

But this need not be, except in the experience of those who do not know the truth. Once you have been taught that there is no power external to you and that the only power is the power of God within you, from that moment on you begin to be free of the world's hypnotism, the world's suggestions, and you can protect yourself from these.

You do not protect yourself, as Paul did, from a carnal mind that is "enmity against God," but you do protect yourself from that carnal mind which is a *belief* in two powers. Immediately upon awakening in the morning, your very first thought must be to protect yourself from the universal belief in two powers. This belief is within you only because you have accepted it from the world. You are free of it when you consciously come out from among those who believe in two powers and make yourself entirely separate from them through your understanding, first of all, of God as one power, all power, the only power, and then that all this power is within you.

The power of God flows out from you, and It enfolds everyone who comes within reach of your consciousness. No power flows to you: no good power and no bad power. All power is given unto you from God; it is within you; and it flows out from you, but you must open out a way for it to escape. You are the one who first must acknowledge:

> The kingdom of God is within me, and the
> kingdom of God is the all-power, the only power,
> the all-mighty power. Besides It there are no
> other powers: no material and no mental powers,
> for the only real power is the power of Spirit,
> the power of Soul, the invisible power that is
> within me and is forever flowing forth from
> me to embrace this world.

All the evil in this world operates as material or mental powers, or as persons. If you lump them all together as carnal mind, illusion, or hypnotism, and see them as of non-power, with the realization that you embody the only power there is and that all the Father has is yours, then these suggestions will not come nigh your household. They will not come nigh your consciousness. Nothing can enter "that defileth. . . or maketh a lie,"[11] if you are standing guard with the realization of one power, because all there is besides that one power is a universal belief in two powers, and you must consciously reject it.

When you perceive that the only evil there is in the world is operating as a belief in two powers, functioning as material or mental law or power, or as person, and that all of this is really only a belief in two powers and that it is not power, for *I* in the midst of you is the only power, then you shut your mind off from being an antenna for the suggestions of the world.

How Life Becomes Conditioned

The mind—your mind—acts in two ways. It is first of all the substance of your physical sense of body. Your physical sense of body is not made up of matter: it is made up of mind, which in its particular form we call matter. Your mind is the essence and the substance of your physical sense of body, and your mind in its *pure* state is an unconditioned mind: it knows neither good nor evil; it has no qualities whatsoever. It is like God, Spirit. God is infinite, eternal, immortal being. God is neither good nor bad. God is infinity. God is immortality. God is life, but God is not long life or short life, healthy life or diseased life.

God is just pure life with no qualifications whatsoever, and this is also true of your mind, when mind is understood to be a transparency for Consciousness. Then your mind, which is the substance of your body, is unconditioned, and your body is immortal and eternal. Your body has no qualities of good or of evil. It has no qualities of health or disease. It has no qualities of strength or weakness. It is unconditioned mind formed, a mind that is the transparency for Spirit, Consciousness. What determines the nature of your life is what you accept in mind, for this becomes the conditioning that appears as your body, as your business, as your home, as your family.

> I know that God is "closer. . . than breathing, and nearer than hands and feet." I know that the king-dom of God is within me. I know that all power is within me, and that this power is God, and It is not a power over something. It is Itself infinite all-power.

> My life is the God-life expressing Itself as my individual life, and therefore I have no short life or long life; I have no young life or old life; I have no sick life or well life; I have no moral life or immoral life: I have only the unconditioned life which is God.

Unconditioning the Mind

In your work take all the synonyms for God you can remember that will bring to your conscious realization the truth that *I* in the midst of you will never leave you or forsake you:

> *I* within me is my bread, wine, and water:
> I need not look to "man, whose breath is in his
> nostrils."[12] I need not put my faith in "princes."
> I need not look outside my own being, for *I* will
> never leave me or forsake me. *I* will be with me
> unto the end of the world, and *I* am my bread.
> *I* embody my meat and wine and water.
> In fact, *I* embody the power of resurrection,
> so that even the lost years of the locust
> will be restored unto me.

In this way you are filling your mind with truth, embodying truth in your mind, and this becomes the substance or the conditioning of your life, mind, body, and business. That is the only conditioning that your mind should have, the conditioning that comes from the *I* that you are. *I* within you imparts unto your mind, truth, and thus the mind performs a second function as a reflector. What you fill your mind with reflects as your material sense of body, business, home, family, and all human relationships. *I* imparts to your mind the truth of being, and the mind reflects that throughout your being, body, and entire life. In doing this, you have shut yourself off from the world's suggestion that there are two powers.

Helping to Dissolve World Appearances

If we were to leave our homes and work, and all the problems of the world, and were to found some kind of transcendentalist colony, live together joyously, happily, and peacefully for a time, and walk out on the beautiful countryside, exclaiming over its peace, we would not solve any problems but would be running away from New York, Chicago, Los Angeles, and San Francisco, or any other community with its troubles, hiding our heads in the sand and saying, "How lovely it is! We are all at peace"—as if we really could be while anybody out in the world was fighting.

It is literally true that if there is a starving man in the world, we cannot really be rich. If there is a sick man in the world, we cannot be wholly well. Why? We are all part of one another. We are fulfilling our function only when we stay out in the world with the truth we know, and prove that through this truth we can benefit those who are still in ignorance of it. Because the news in the paper today may sound bad, we should not think how lovely it would be if we could run away to some remote place and not be aware of the world's problems. It would not be that way at all. The beautiful part is that, knowing this truth, we can stay in the midst of the world's problems and play a part in dissolving the appearance.

Widening the Circle

When I bring to my mind the truth of being, the truth of God as my real being and the only power, all within me, and at the same time realize that all that exists as an appearance is the carnal mind, the "arm of flesh," of no power, I help to dissolve that picture - first for myself, so that my own life begins to show forth some measure of the harmonies to which it is entitled. Later, others see it, and I begin to perceive that the truth operates for their benefit, also.

Then this circle widens and widens, so that as we stay in this world and face the appearances, we help to dissolve them. How is that possible? None of these evils or dangers is externalized. They exist as mental images in the mind of man, and only those who know this truth can help to dissolve them. If, for example, an individual brings his problems to me or a thousand bring their problems to me, I, being one with God, with truth, am a majority. If I know that these claims of human sense are not externalized conditions, that they have no real existence, existing only as the belief in two powers, mental projections in thought, projected out on the screen of life, but having no externalized reality or form or substance or law, I soon find that there is healing.

When we face a storm at sea, as the Master did, with the realization that there is no externalized storm, because this is a mental image stemming from the universal belief in two powers, then the bubble bursts, and the storm subsides. We have witnessed this with destructive forces of nature and through this truth have seen them dissolve. Evil does not exist as an externalized condition or person. It exists only as *maya,* illusion, carnal mind, hypnotism, appearance—any name we like, as long as we understand that it means a mental image in thought that has no externalized form, no substance, and no law.

Removing the Fear of Death From Disease

The healing of disease is not as difficult as it seems. If, as an individual, you can come to the realization that death itself is not a power, that death cannot separate you from the life of God, the soul of God, the consciousness of God, what difference does death make? When you come to that realization, you have overcome ninety percent of the diseases of this world. Actually, if you could demonstrate it, you would prove that it is one hundred percent, because the only reason an illness is serious is the fear of death.

Take the fear of death out of disease, and disease would have no sting; it would have no power whatsoever. But you cannot take the fear out of disease as long as you believe it leads to death and that death is something to be avoided.

Someday death will have to be met, and you might as well meet it now, while you do not have to meet it in that earthly sense of death, but meet it here and now with the realization that death has never separated anyone from the love of God. What has happened to all the saints, sages, seers, and spiritually gifted people of all ages, if death could destroy them or anyone else?

No, it could not be possible for so much human sacrifice to be on the face of the earth, for so many men and women to have given themselves and their lives to the world, and then feel that death has suddenly cut them off and brought something horrible to them. It did not do that at all. Death was merely another stage in their experience. When you come to view death in that manner, you will have destroyed most disease, because disease has its basis in that fear. That is undoubtedly the reason that certain diseases are more difficult to meet than other claims, because the claim of some diseases is so immediately connected with the fear of death, bringing with them a sense of inevitability.

To understand that even though I "walk through the valley of the shadow of death,"[13] God, as the *I* that I am, will be walking with me, would make me absolutely indifferent to the experience of death, and being indifferent to it, would also postpone it. Is it not usually the things we fear that come upon us?

It Is Your Choice

What you entertain in your mind is what you experience, and what you entertain in your mind that appears as discord or disease is just the belief in two powers. What form that takes is different with different individuals. To some it brings disease. But regardless of the form, it is still only the belief in two powers. If you sufficiently instruct the mind in truth, you will find that your mind is not an antenna. There can then be no room for the belief in two powers in any form to enter, to defile, or to make a lie.

Actually we do choose each day whether we will serve God or mammon. We choose each day whether we will serve spirit, the one power, or the belief in two powers. We are suffering from nothing more than these hypnotic suggestions, which we do not have to see or hear in order to take them in. They act upon us hypnotically as suggestion. Only they do not have to be directed at us; we pick them up from the atmosphere.

Our work then, is to prevent as much evil from entering our mind as possible. That we do through our conscious rejection of the belief in two powers and our conscious acceptance of the truth that the presence and power of God is within us, and Its name is *I.*

> *I* in the midst of me is mighty.
> *I* in the midst of
> me is my bread, wine, and water. *I* in the
> midst of me is my resurrection.

> As I put on the whole armor of God and attain
> the realization of God, no world belief can
> enter to defile or make a lie.

Being Consciously Alive

There are three parts of you. There is you, yourself, that which you call *I.* This is the sum total of your whole being, and it is divided into stages of awareness. So we have *I,* the *I* that you are, which is your God-being, Soul, Spirit. Then there is your mind and there is your body. Your mind serves a function in two ways: as your avenue of awareness and as the substance of your body, your business, your relationships, and of everything that concerns you.

Because your mind is imbued with the truth you know,

your mind imbued with truth becomes the substance of the form of your body and your business. The acceptance into your mind of the universal belief in two powers manifests itself as sin, disease, death, lack, limitation, all forms of discordant living.

To be a follower of the Master you will continually be coming up against his statement that the way is strait and narrow and few there be that enter. There are few who wish to dedicate themselves to conscious knowing, conscious studying, conscious pondering, and conscious meditating. Since life is consciousness, those who are unwilling to be actively conscious all the time are the living dead. They are walking around in a dream, not aware of where they are going, or why, or even what is influencing them to go, come, do, or be.

Part of the tragedy of human living is the amount of time that is spent in wasted energy. There is room and time for legitimate entertainment, vacations, holidays, the theater, and for television, but not to the extent of ceasing to be a conscious, living person, not a person who walks around influenced by every wind that blows, but a person who influences, not by consciously dominating, but by consciously being a center of God action.

The body itself is a very live piece of mechanism, because mind is its substance. The body itself is of a joyous, vigorous, and vital nature, but not the body that is allowed to walk around without any conscious direction from us. The body must be governed by truth. "Ye shall know the truth, and the truth shall make you free"[14] of all discords, all inharmonies, all inequalities, because you are setting the law in motion through conscious realization.

As a matter of fact, you are going beyond that. You are letting yourself be governed by Grace. You are denying the power of material and mental laws, so that only God's grace, centered in the *I* that is your true being, your real identity, God's grace functioning as *I*, lives your life.

Live on the Grace of Today

There is no need to take thought, no need to be concerned or anxious because at the right moment it is God, or Truth, which thinks or gives to us the thoughts we think. God's thoughts are not man's thoughts, and man's thoughts are not God's thoughts. As we become more and more receptive to the inflow of God's thoughts, we are God-governed. That is why in our work we devote so much time to that listening ear, to making ourselves receptive, not merely to thoughts which we already know, but to new thoughts.

We do not live on yesterday's manna, and we do not live on yesterday's truth. We do not live on yesterday's treatments. We do not live on yesterday's idea of how to conduct a business. Business can change overnight; the nature of it can change overnight.

In every phase of life, do not try to live on yesterday's manna. Do not learn formulas and repeat them each day. Act as though you had entrance to the kingdom of God and could go to God any minute, any second, any hour for fresh illumination and for fresh guidance, for fresh instruction, or instruction in different ways or new ways. Never be satisfied with the truth you knew yesterday. God is infinite. Truth is infinite, so we have no need of anything that we had yesterday. Infinity is pouring Itself through today. Understanding that, the study of truth does not become stale. It is always appearing in fresh forms. We do not have to go over the same lesson day after day. We do not have to go over the same books day after day.

There is no loss if some days we skip reading or hearing truth, because we are making room for Truth to reveal Itself to us within ourselves. We must make time when we do not live in the books or in the tapes. We must make time for saying, "God, You spoke to that man. You can speak to me. If You speak to anyone on the earth, You can speak to me."

"God is no respecter of persons."¹⁵ To God there is no high or low. To God there is no rich or poor. To God there is no such thing as a religion. God forbid that you ever find a religion in heaven. There would be no disgrace on anyone's part if he threw every teaching out of the window and said, "God, I don't believe any of them unless it comes to me directly from You." There would be no harm in that, no loss in that, because no teaching is so important that a better one cannot come to you if you listen to God.

God is infinite, and "God is no respecter of persons." Sometime ago somebody complained to me that learning about truth is too expensive. And I told that person that it does not have to cost a penny. No one has to buy books or go to classes. If a person wants truth, let him go home and stay there and make God talk to him. It might take a while. It might take a year or two or three. But it is worth it and it will be without price.

Reading books and going to classes is the easier and more expeditious way. But the other is a possible way, because "God is no respecter of persons." If you insist, if you knock, if you seek, the answer will come. But it will come from within you from an infinite center, an infinite storehouse that is already within you, just waiting for you to open out the doors to release it.

The Harmony of Your Life
Is Locked Up Within You

Your health, your supply, your companionship, and your home are all locked up within you. The moment you realize that the *I* of your being embodies these and that It flows out into expression, it will be that way unto you, instead of having it come from some outside source, or some "man, whose breath is in his nostrils," "princes," favoritism, or any other external way.

There is the *I* that I am, and the truth that I know is that with which I am unconditioning my mind. That unconditioning appears as the harmony of my entire existence. If I do not know the truth consciously, the world is pouring its beliefs into my mind subliminally and through the press, radio, and television. And this then manifests itself as the conditioning of my mind and the appearance of my body.

Evil is impersonal, and you must never attach it to person, place, thing, circumstance, or condition. It reaches you impersonally through suggestion in one way or another. But the evil is always a belief in two powers. You always handle it as an impersonal suggestion from the carnal mind and drop it.

When the Master said, "Get thee behind me, Satan,"[16] he was not facing a physical, external devil. He was facing a suggestion within himself. And he knew enough to say, "Get thee behind me, Satan." And then Satan just toddled away!

Across The Desk

Spiritual attainment cannot be judged by outer forms. For example, wealth cannot be equated with spirituality since it may be the reaping of good human sowing, resulting in abundance.

Many persons in the religious world, however, mistakenly assume that poverty and spirituality are synonymous, believing that poverty is the badge of spiritual attainment. Yet the Master clearly pointed out that his ministry was to reveal the abundant life: "I am come that they might have life and that they might have it more abundantly."

How could it be otherwise since spiritual principles reveal the omnipresence of all good flowing forth into form out of the infinite divine consciousness, expressing as individual consciousness? In proportion as greater awareness of our true being as unlimited consciousness becomes ours, is it not natural for it to manifest as all things necessary, with the twelve basketsful left over to share? A measure of spiritual consciousness brings with it the sufficiency of omnipresent Grace.

Chapter Eight

The Fruitage of Knowing
God Aright

If you think there is a God external to you, you are not living at-one with God. To understand God aright, you must know that God is in the midst of you, not separate and apart from you. God is not to be gained, won, or searched after. God is to be recognized as the one Self. When you understand that God is really your Self, then that *I* which you declare your Self to be is really God-being, the offspring of God, that is, God individualized, God in individual expression.

Your Divine Inheritance of Sonship

When you know that God is individual being, you do not look outside yourself. Rather you relax within yourself: God is closer to you than breathing, and you do not have to go to God for anything, for God knows your need before you do. It is not God in heaven that knows you have need of things: it is God in the midst of you that knows your need, "Your Father knoweth that ye have need of these things. . . for it is your Father's good pleasure to give you the kingdom."[1] You do not earn it. You do not deserve it. In fact, nobody could be good enough to deserve God's grace. But it is yours by right of inheritance. The *I* of your being is the Christ, or the son of God, and It is heir of God and joint-heir. So whether you earn it or deserve it has nothing to do with the fact that as the son of God you cannot be disinherited.

I know of a woman who married against the wishes of her very wealthy parents. The man she married had a great deal of money, so she had no concern about money. But when her mother and father passed on, she learned that she had been disinherited. She paid no attention to this because as far as the money was concerned it meant nothing to her. There was a particular Persian rug, however, which had been promised to her, and she had looked forward to owning it some day. Two years after the passing of her parents, she remembered the rug and thought, "Well, probably my sister will let me have that rug, so I will write my lawyer to get in touch with her." When the lawyer contacted the sister, her response was, "No, Mother did not want her to have it, and she is not going to have it. She has been disinherited."

That triggered something in the consciousness of the disinherited woman, "Disinherited? God disinherit His child? I do not believe it. God cannot disinherit His children, and God is the only parent. I just cannot believe that it could happen." She wrote her lawyer to find out what the provisions of the will were. When the lawyer searched the records, he found that there was no will recorded, and upon contacting the family lawyer, he was told, "Why, of course. The will was probated on such and such a day. I remember it distinctly, but I cannot find a record of it." And there was no record of it. So the family lawyer began a search and found the will under the blotter of his desk where his clerk had placed it because he had something else to do and had forgotten it. It turned out that the will never had been probated but when it was, the woman was given her rug and many other things, too, not because she wanted a rug, but because she was living spiritually and demonstrated spiritually.

No one can violate spiritual living and then demonstrate spiritual good. No one can walk around talking about how good or how bad his mother and father are and then demonstrate spiritual abundance. There is a need on the part of everyone to live spiritually, and then he can observe how spiritual living governs his business, his inheritance, and everything else that concerns his affairs.

To live spiritually, however, you must know the nature of God. Unless you know that God is the only parent, you will not be living spiritually. You will be living according to the human belief that you have a mother and father on earth. You could either benefit or suffer in accordance with whether they happened to be good or bad, generous or miserly, rich or poor.

If, while respecting their human parents, individuals would get over some of their slushy sentimentality and realize that God is really the parent, the creative, maintaining, and sustaining principle, they could then be affectionate on the human level and yet not put their parents in the false light of being parents when they are not really parents but human caretakers. God, the Father, is the creative principle.

God Knows Your Need

Unless you know to a point of conviction that your heavenly Father within you already knows your need and that it is His good pleasure to give you the kingdom, you cannot live spiritually in the area of supply. You will continually be looking to "man, whose breath is in his nostrils,"[2] and if it is not a parent to whom you are looking, it will be to a wife, a husband, or a child. When all these fail, you may have to turn to a cold government and ask it to take over and give you your pittance. And why will it be necessary for you to take such a step? Because instead of living spiritually, which means living in the realization that there is a He within and that it is His good pleasure to give you the kingdom, you have decided to live by the human standard that good comes by earthly means through earthly people. When you are convinced that the Father knows your

126 The Art of Spiritual Living

needs before you do, your prayer changes and you live and pray spiritually, which means never going to the Father *for* anything, but rather *with* something: with love, confidence, assurance, remembrance, and realization.

Forget the Fulfillment of Self in Service to God and Man

Persons who live humanly are always going places or doing things to *get* something from somebody. On the other hand, those who live spiritually enjoy not only an abundance, but twelve basketsful left over. Their main function in life is to serve, to give, to share, to cooperate. The getting comes by reflected action. In other words, the bread they cast upon the water comes back to them, and always comes back multiplied. A person living spiritually does not look for it to come back, but forgets self. "Greater love hath no man than this, that a man lay down his life for his friends."[3] Always spiritual living is founded upon a forgetfulness of self in service to God and man.

It should be noted, however, that it is possible to appear to be fulfilling that principle and at the same time be violating it. As the Master pointed out, even though a person may go out and do a tremendous amount of benevolence and charity, if he calls attention to himself so as to receive man's thanks, praise, gratitude, and recognition, he loses God's grace. The only grace that comes to a person lies in the good he does that is unknown, in that which he does silently, secretly.

"Thy Father which seeth in secret himself shall reward thee openly."[4] This Father is closer to you than breathing. You cannot fool Him, because He is your self. He is your intelligence; He is your wisdom; He is the very guiding instinct of your being.

God is at the center of your being, and the moment you violate a spiritual principle, you are out of tune with It. Violating a spiritual principle does not necessarily mean sinning

in the world's understanding of sinning. Only when you silently and secretly realize that your real parent is not your earthly
father but God within you, are you in tune with the Infinite.
You are living spiritually when your life reflects the fact that you
are consciously aware that all the Father has is yours, instead of
merely making affirmations about it, which is not going to do
anything for anybody, but rather knowing it to the point of realization. That is spiritual living, spiritual living carried into every
phase of life—your home life, business life, church life—a life
which brings that everlasting peace that passes understanding.

Requisites for Living the Spiritual Life

Being able to live the spiritual life is dependent upon your
knowing, first of all, that God is your selfhood and the selfhood
of everyone you meet, and then on your knowing that the
Father within you knows your need, so that you do not have to
take time telling Him about it. Rather you must know that it is
His good pleasure to give you the kingdom, and you can rest
and relax in that assurance. When you have that assurance, you
are really living the spiritual life.

It is important to realize that this God upon whom you are
relying is not something external to you or separate and apart
from you, but is your own selfhood under the name of *I*. That
I, which is at the center of your being, which you call yourself,
that *I*, which you are, is really the offspring of God, God individualized, the Christ, or son of God, which is heir to all the
heavenly riches. Abide in that word, never looking out here,
performing every task that is given you to do, doing your work
every day, not running away to hide from the world, but doing
all things that are given you to do without any thought of result
or reward, relying always on *I* within you, not for a reward but
to open your eyes to the kingdom within.

It is dangerous to accept the belief of a God that punishes
and rewards. God does not punish and God does not reward.

Whatever God does, God merely does as a function of God. You might liken it to the sun and sunlight. The sun does not shine and give light and warmth as a reward to anybody for anything. To shine is its function, and it cannot withhold sunshine, not even from the sinner. God is not a human being. God does not act like a human parent or a judge on the bench. Not at all! God is infinite being and is forever being infinite being. God cannot give and God cannot withhold. God can only *be.* Your knowing this truth brings that God-being into active experience in your life. All you are called upon to know is the truth about God and to relax in God.

God as Being

Now you come to what is probably the most difficult part of all for most students. It is the custom to speak of God as the one power and the all-power, not realizing that God as the one power means that God is not a power. For God to be a power would indicate that God is a power *over* some other power or *against* some other power. But God is not a power over any other power or against any other power, because there are no other powers.

So, rightly understood, God is not a power: God is being. God is always being God, and there is no power being exercised, because if there were, it would certainly have to be exercised on something, over something, against something, or for something. But God has nothing to do anything for, about, or against. God is always love, and love is not love over anything: love is just love. God is intelligence, but intelligence is not a power over anything: intelligence is just intelligence. Life is not over anything: there is no life over death, because death does not exist as a reality. That Jesus could raise them from the dead is proof that death is not a power. God is not a power over disease, because disease is not a reality.

Praying to God to heal your patient is not in accordance

with Infinite Way principles. True, a healing may actually be brought about that way, but it will not be because God had anything to do with it. It will be because your faith was being fulfilled. You could have had just as much faith in some religious medal or some saint's bones, and it would have done the work. All such things embody some manner of healing.

There are a few people who pray to God for health and get it—not many, but here and there a few. It is not from God. If God ever answered anyone's prayer to heal anyone, God would be a monster. What! God answer my prayer to heal you, and leave all the other people unhealed? That is like praising God for stopping the war on the European front, while war was going on in the Japanese arena. Can God do half a job? No, if God were in the business of stopping wars, there would never have been one started in the first place. Wars just go on until a nation runs out of ammunition or food, and then the war stops.

You Cannot Use God

When the truth that you cannot use God begins to dawn in your consciousness, you are beginning to live spiritually. As long as you think that you can use God, you are holding yourself superior to God, as if you could tell God what He should be doing to this poor soul, as if you had more love in your heart for him than God has, and as if you were urging God to use power on his behalf.

The beginning of spiritual wisdom is when you know the nature of God, and you do not know that while you think you know better than God what should be done, believe there is something you can tell God, or that God can do something for one individual that God is not doing equally for everybody. "God is no respecter of persons."[5]

God is not a power to be used; God is not a power that destroys your enemies. God is not going to enslave anybody for your sake. Once you understand that it could not be a part of God's nature to do evil to anyone, you would know the futility of praying to God to have your enemy harmed or to have him lose a war.

Business as a Spiritual Activity

This same mistaken idea as to the nature of God is evident in the business world. How may people pray for success in a business venture, knowing full well that if their prayers are answered, it will be at the loss of their competitor. That is not praying, and there is no God listening to such prayer. Instead of trying to gain business at the expense of a competitor, there would be better business for everyone if competitors could agree to put their heads together in the attitude, "How can we give better service and increase the amount of business in this neighborhood?" Do not believe for a minute that God prospers one person's business at somebody else's expense.

It is easy to bring business under the jurisdiction of spiritual activity. Business is not separate and apart from one's spiritual experience. Business is as spiritual as any form of living, just as spiritual as going to church or as engaging in prayer. Not all forms of business would fit into that category, but business, as I understand it, is really a part of spiritual living.

Forgiveness as the Foundation for a Life Work

In the very first year of the great depression of the 1930's, a man who had made a fortune in the building business lost his entire business and fortune. His wife had to go to work, and he took what seemed like a menial job and was having a very difficult time with it. One day that man came to my office and asked for help. Owing to conditions, there seemed to be no way for him to meet the problem except the possibility of collecting a large sum of money owed him. If he could collect that, he and his wife could live out the depression and wait for conditions to improve. He wanted me to help him collect that money through metaphysical means.

My reply was, "There is no provision whatsoever for collecting a debt spiritually. That should in no wise interfere with your supply, however, or the amount of it, for the simple reason that God is omnipresence and God is infinite. Supply therefore must be infinite and omnipresent, which means that it must be where you are. The blessing is that it is not dependent on 'man, whose breath is in his nostrils.' It is not dependent on any man's favors. Business is an activity of God and has nothing whatsoever to do with any man except that he is an instrument for the showing forth of God's business." "Well, then, what am I to do?"

"The first step would be to forgive your debtor! You need not tell the man you have forgiven the debt. Forgive it within yourself, within your heart. If the time comes when he wishes to pay it or can pay it, that will be his demonstration. But your demonstration is to forgive it. And then, not looking to yesterday's manna, let us see what happens with God today."

It should not be difficult for you to imagine how such an idea was received in the light of the vast sum of money that this man had looked upon as his last hope. But that very night he received a call from a real estate man, saying that a particular piece of property which had a peculiar shape could be sold if some way could be found to use it as a site for a factory. He was asked to look at it and give them some advice. So he went down the next morning, looked at it, advised them, and received a check that not only paid up his own personal debts, but gave him enough to live on for a few more weeks. The following week he received a call from a church asking if he had had anything to do with the plans that had been drawn ten years before to build the church. To his affirmative response, he was told, "Well, we are ready, so come down now."

Even that was not all. It was really pressed down and running over. The next day he received a call from Washington, together with a check for expenses to go to New York for consultation on a government housing development. Within two years that man was admitted to partnership in the firm that was building government projects. Was it business or was it spiritual living, obeying the spiritual laws of scripture, that brought forth these developments?

This sort of thing I have witnessed in many types of business activity, whether in the marketing of a product or in relationships between corporations and labor. In whatever way these principles have been practiced, they have proved to be effective, not by trying to change a particular business situation, but by introducing spiritual principles into the business. The principle involved is brought out clearly in two chapters on human relationships: "Love Thy Neighbor" in *Practicing the Presence,*[6] and "The Relationship of Oneness" in *The Art of Spiritual Healing.*[7]

When you perceive that God is the one Self and you begin to realize that you are the same individual that I am, and that "I and my Father are one"[8] is just as true of you as it is of me, then we begin to dwell in harmony. As long as there are contracts in the business world or the material world, however, I suppose we will go through the form of making contracts.

Actually there should be no necessity for those things. In work such as ours there should be no need for contracts because the only real bond between students on the spiritual path is a spiritual one. In supporting the activity of the Infinite Way, there is no dependence on memberships, no urging to have students attend lectures or classes and no requests for contributions: weekly, monthly, or yearly. The spiritual law is the law of supply. It is not dependent on princes: it is dependent only on the presence and the activity of the Christ, the spiritual presence in individual consciousness.

A New Approach to Salesmanship

Once you realize that He that is within you is greater than he that is in the world, that He performs that which is given you to do and perfects that which concerns you, and you attain the consciousness that there is a He within you, then this He, this presence, this infinite invisible, goes before you to "make the crooked places straight."[9] It is That which goes before you to be the cement of your relationships.

When I was a salesman there was one man in Kansas City to whom I never could sell any merchandise. He was determined that he was not going to buy from me, and for many years he did not. On one trip before I went to that store I looked up a practitioner in the town who said to me, "Well, it is not a question of whether that man buys from you or not. It is only a question as to whether human will and human domination have any place in the spiritual life. As a spiritual being he can be subject only to the same spiritual power as you are. The whole thing comes down to whether or not you believe that there can be another power handling any man." With those words he threw the problem right back at me and not at the man.

When I went into the store that morning and for no reason the man said, "No," I replied, "It seems surprising to me that a man as successful as you are could for so many years refuse to look at the line of a man who is as successful as I am. My merchandise has a reputation for style and quality, and you do not even know what has made that reputation."

He said, "You are right. When can we have an appointment?"

Was that business or was that spiritual living? I had been violating spiritual living. I was seeing that man as a man with a will and a mind of his own, and not even a pleasant one. Therefore it was not he but I who was doing the malpracticing. The minute I released him from that belief he was a cooperative man.

To me business really is not business. Business is spiritual living or at least one facet of spiritual living. Whether it is business, marriage, spiritual teaching, school teaching, or anything else, it really is just a matter of spiritual living. And that is all it is.

Bringing the Divine Government Into Your Activity

I had the pleasure one time of working with a schoolteacher who was having the usual trouble in New England of bad weather all winter, which resulted in so many absences from school during January, February, and March that every term several pupils were not promoted. I worked with that schoolteacher throughout a whole summer vacation. When she returned to school in the fall, she had the experience of going through January, February, and March with only five percent absenteeism when the average was something like twenty or twenty-three percent. At the end of the term not one student was retained. That teacher who had never gone any further than normal school went on from there and eventually received her doctorate and was given a special appointment by the State of Massachusetts to travel throughout the world to learn and bring back new ideas on education.

Her activity at school was really a spiritual activity, knowing the children in the school were not children of parents, but children of the one Father, the Father in heaven. She realized that they had only the mind of God, the life of God, the health of God, and that they were not subject to weather, climate, or germs. They were subject to God's government and jurisdiction. It is only necessary to behold that out in front of you to have it reflected back to you.

Whether it is in a public school classroom or an Infinite Way classroom you get what you give. When you behold God as individual being, as the mind of man, as the life and the soul, and are willing to look through human failings, you will have taken the burden of human guilt from every shoulder, and everyone will feel it and respond to you. They think you are very loving, and humanly you are not that at all. It is only that spiritually you are knowing the truth, which is a spiritual way of life. Ultimately that is how the lamb will lie down with the lion. When you perceive that the mind of a lion and the mind of a lamb are the same mind, not two minds, you will bring it forth in demonstration.

All things are possible to spiritual living. And business is not really business. It is a form of spiritual living, if you bring your business into your spiritual life and do not separate them. The same principles that apply in getting along with persons in your family or getting along with your neighbors apply in getting along with all others.

When you go out of a door, stop for a minute. Stop being a human being and try to realize that those you see and those you meet are the same selfhood that you yourself are. They are divine being, God in individual form, regardless of what they may seem to be humanly. Go through this same procedure as you go up or down in an elevator, as you walk out on the street, as you go into a restaurant, and then as you return to your office or shop. In this way your business life will be a facet of your spiritual life.

To Benefit From Prayer, You Must Live According to God's Law

To pray spiritually means never to pray selfishly, never to pray for your own gain or your own benefit, but to make your prayer a realization of God's lovingness: universally and equally. Would that give abundance to everyone? No, because those who are living in violation of the law of love could not benefit from it if someone prayed for them from now until doomsday. Your prayers cannot benefit the person who is in violation of God's law. That explains the lack of healings in many cases. You may wonder why someone is not being healed, not really knowing that inside he may be living in violation of some law of God. The only way you could benefit such a person is if your prayers could awaken him and put him on the spiritual path. Then the healing could follow.

If your prayer or treatment is aimed merely at healing some person's physical discords, you will largely fail, because the physical discords are merely the externalization of a false state of consciousness. It may not be an evil one. It may just be an ignorance of spiritual law. It may be that very difference between being a taker and being a giver.

Giving, Not Taking

It is sad to witness the number of people religiously inclined who indulge in begging. True, it may be for a very good cause, but they are begging for it whatever the cause is. They are trying to get, get, get. That is not the law of God. There is no provision for begging in the law of God, none whatsoever. There is no justification for it and actually no need of it when a person accepts his responsibility and realizes: "I and my Father are one." As long as I live in the realization of God as knowing my need before I do and of God as supplying it as His good pleasure, as long as I am not looking to "man, whose breath is in his nostrils," but to the Father within me to be the presence to go before me, then in some way everything that will support any activity in which I am engaged will appear.

If you want to support activities, you can support them without their sponsors coming to you and begging for what their needs are. After looking at your community or the neighborhood where you live and becoming aware of its needs, whether it is the Y.M.C.A., a hospital, or some other constructive community activity, you should provide your share and thereby take away the need for begging. You also take from yourself the probability of your ever having a need, because your own need is met in your giving, not in receiving.

That lesson came home to me one night sitting in a Christian Science Church, looking up on the wall and seeing the statement: "Divine Love always has met and always will meet every human need." Knowing most of the people in the church, I looked around and thought, "It isn't so. I know too many here who have been waiting years and years for that divine love to meet their need, and it just hasn't happened." Then I found myself wondering why that particular message had been chosen. All of a sudden the meaning of those words dawned on me as I realized that the people in the church were reading those words backwards. The divine love that meets every need is not out here. It is inside. Therefore, it is the divine love you express that meets your need. There is no God out here meeting your need. God is within you, but as long as you are not expressing that divine love, it is unexpressed, and as long as it is unexpressed, it cannot meet your human need.

What constitutes divine love? Forgiveness, charity, benevolence, kindness, cooperativeness, sharing: all these constitute divine love. If you are not expressing divine love, it is not going to return to you or meet your need. It was that awareness that brought a change in my way of life, because I saw how foolish it is to sit around waiting for God to do something.

Are You an Instrument for God's Love?

God is forever being God, so there is no use waiting for God to do something tomorrow. God is already doing it. The question is: Are you an instrument through which God's work is being done? Are you an instrument as which God is functioning? Certainly not while you are sitting around waiting for divine love to move on the face of the waters. You are being an instrument, as God's wisdom, intelligence, love, and life find expression through you.

Life stops functioning for you when you say, "What's the use? There's nothing ahead." The moment life stops functioning, you are like the chicken who has had its head cut off. You wiggle around for a little while, but you are dead. That is why there are so many living dead on earth. They have given up. They are not living. They are not expressing. They are not enjoying. They are not sharing. They are not being. They are not cooperating. They are not letting themselves be instruments for God. They have just become dead weights waiting for a God to make them happy, prosperous, or successful. And they are dead. Their lives are finished even though there may be years ahead of them.

God is living your life, but you are the transparency for that only while you are letting that Life live Itself as you. Your life at any moment could be outwardly a blank. Something may come up which might divest you of your money, your health, or your business. The question is: Do you jump out of a window? Do you wait for the undertaker to come along? Or do you get up the next day, brush off your clothes, and start over again, letting God live by beginning to give—even if you have nothing left to give but something off your own back?

Looking to God for something is ignorance of what God is. There is no spiritual living on that basis. Spiritual living begins with your knowing the truth, and the truth you have to know is the truth about God. God is not a power: God is being. God is the creative principle, the maintaining and sustaining principle. But God is not being a power *over* anything. God is merely power in expression.

As long as you are aware of omnipresence or immanuel, God with us, you never need to pray for anything, because Immanuel is the presence of God, which is the health of your countenance, the cement of your relationships, your bread, wine, water, your safety and security, your abundance, and your peace that passes understanding. Even though there are snares and delusions in the world, and pitfalls, they will not come nigh your dwelling place.

There are times when you can be a temporary help to your neighbor, and that is usually when they ask for it and thereby bring themselves into accord with spiritual law. When a person is brought to an illumined consciousness, that illumined consciousness can be of some temporary help to him, but not permanently, because the moment he goes back to his sins, his material way of living, his ignorance of God, worse things will come upon him, unless he is willing that his consciousness be raised. Very often you will help people who want to be rid of their pains, diseases, or sins. But if they are not eager to fill their consciousness with God, they have just been left with a vacuum, and some other discord will hop into it before long.

The theme of this *Letter* has been the importance of the nature, the being, and the function of God. When you understand that, you need take no thought for what you will eat or what you will drink. You need take no thought! Just do those things each day that are given you to do, and He that is within you will perfect it.

ACROSS THE DESK

The consciousness that can be a light to those who dwell in the darkness of material sense comes as a gift of Grace, a gift which is ours because of an inner preparation that may have been made either in some earlier lifetime or in this particular experience. Preceding it there is that hungering and thirsting after God, evidenced by a willingness to leave all to follow the Christ which has knocked for eons of time at the door of consciousness.

One of the most important forms that preparation can take is practicing the principles of spiritual living and healing. Through the practice of the presence and inner alertness required to reinterpret appearances—good or bad—as they are presented to him, the student becomes more and more aware of the presence of God and of the nature of this world as the appearance-world, thereby preparing himself for the descent of that Grace which is sufficient to every need.

To this end, a study of "The Consciousness of Truth Is the Healer," in *Consciousness Is What I Am* is recommended and will be of inestimable value in opening consciousness to receive the gift.

Chapter Nine

The Consciousness
of the Individual

What you learn about God is the truth about your own consciousness, for God constitutes your consciousness. To learn about God separate and apart from individual consciousness will only tend to separate you from your good. Belief or faith in God has its place, and it may eventually lead some persons to greater awareness, but it is not a good thing at this stage of your unfoldment. So unless you can also realize oneness, or at-one-ment, when you think of God you will have God outside of you.

As long as God is a word in your mind, there is no use in praying, because you cannot get an answer from a word in your mind, a word which represents merely a concept. Even if you change the word God into such words as "Mind", "Life", or "Love", it will continue to be something in your mind about which you are entertaining a concept, and not yourself. If a whole group of persons were to write a paper explaining the meaning of divine love or what divine mind or God is, there would be just as many different concepts of God, Mind, Life, and Love as there were persons, and that would indicate that they did not know God at all or have any real understanding of God.

If there is a you conceiving of a God, thinking of God, hoping for God, searching for God, there is duality and failure. The moment there is the realization, "I Am That I Am,"[1] not "I will be; I long to be; I hope to be: I would like to be worthy of"; then God has become incarnate as individual being: God the Father manifest as God the son, but still just One. God the Father is God the son. Until you can see that *I*, God, am expressing my Self as I-Joel, and therefore all that *I*-God has is I-Joel's, because we are not two but One, you will be missing the mark. Only this realization of oneness can stop you from wanting something or someone external to yourself. As long as there is a want or desire, there is a sense of separation.

Why Desire Is Sin

One of the Infinite Way Wisdoms states that "desire is sin."[2] Why? Is it not because if I desire integrity, am I not acknowledging that I do not have it? If I desire companionship, am I not acknowledging that I do not have it? Even if I desire God, is it not an acknowledgment that I do not have It? All this is sin, because I and the Father are one, and all that the Father has is mine.

As I abide in the Word and let the Word abide in me, I have no desires. I am living only in this moment, conscious of the fact that whatever I need an hour from now will appear, whatever I need tomorrow will appear, whatever I need next year will appear. Why? Because I now embody it. I have meat that the world knows not of.

What I have to do is to be patient, live in this very moment, feel assured that all that the Father has is embodied in me, and that it is unfolding every moment in accordance with my need. If my need this moment is dollars, then those dollars will appear at the moment they are needed, often before that. If my need is transportation, at the right moment it will be waiting for me. Whatever the need is becomes apparent, not because I desire it, not because I want it, not because I need it, but *because I already possess it.*

Those persons who have large freezers with a stock of food in them for a whole month do not put it all on the table at one time. Knowing that it is in the freezer, they are content to bring out only what is necessary at each meal. They do not have to go and look to be sure there is enough for tomorrow, because they know there is enough for the entire month.

Once I know that I and the Father are one, not two, that God is infinite intelligence and therefore must know my needs, that God is divine love and it is His good pleasure to give me the kingdom, it is as if I had an eternal deep freezer, an infinite one. So I need not be concerned for anything more than I need at this particular hour, because whatever it is that is needed in the next hour will unfold from within that infinite storehouse which is the *I* that I am.

Restoring the Lost Years the Locust Has Eaten

Within the *I* that I am is the power of resurrection, so that even if there are some "years that the locust hath eaten,"[3] this power of resurrection will restore those years. It makes no difference how late in life it is. Life is eternal, and life is no older than the life we are living at this moment. We are as young this moment as an infant or as a child of three, because this is the only moment in which we live, and in this moment in which we are living and being, what more can we have? You may say that an infant has a longer future to look forward to. Look around at some of the gravestones, and you will find that some of them did not. They were no more sure of tomorrow at infancy or three years of age than anyone is at thirty.

I can remember that at thirty, thirty-five, or forty, I was less sure of tomorrow than I am today. In the human scale who knows what tomorrow will bring? Spiritually, I cannot be separated from the life of God. I cannot be separated from the love of God. I cannot be separated from the consciousness of God. So the only thing I do not know about tomorrow is in which room I will be living or in which country. But I have lived in so many different places in my lifetime that it does not make any difference.

The only time that counts is this minute. It is in this minute that I am alive, fully alive, and it is this minute in which I am aware of God. It is in this minute that I am aware of an infinite storehouse, and I have witnessed it manifested over the years in whatever form was necessary.

Life is ageless and eternal. As you sit looking out of your eyes, you have a feeling of agelessness. You do not have a feeling of age. Even if you are ill, it does not make you feel old. It is not possible. A person can feel only his life as of this moment, and this moment it is life, and it is life eternal, life immortal, and life abundant.

God as I *Assures Oneness*

"I am come that they might have life, and that they might have it more abundantly."[4]

> This *I* is the I that I am. This *I* in the midst of
> me is here for the specific purpose of living
> my life and living it abundantly.

As long as you can realize that God is that *I* that is within you or that this *I* that is within you is the very Christ of God, the offspring, the heir, one with God, then you can live this minute abundantly. And who can live any other minute abundantly except *this* minute? There is no other minute in which you can live. You cannot live yesterday abundantly; you cannot live tomorrow abundantly. Only in this very moment of Grace can you live abundantly, and only by virtue of the *I* that you are.

And what I are you? You are that *I,* the son of God, heir of God, so much joint-heir that you can say, "He that seeth me seeth him that sent me,"[5] for that *I* that you are and that the Father is are one. But even then you can acknowledge that the Father within you is greater than the personal sense of *I,* because there are two aspects of the *I: I* the Father and I the son. *I* the Father is that invisible area of you which has manifested Itself as individual you. As that *I* individualized, you then have all that that invisible *I* has, because you are heir to all of it. That *I* has been planted in the midst of you that you may have life and that you may have it more abundantly.

When you think of the word God, "divine mind," or "divine love," you are putting God over somewhere separate and apart from your own being. Instead let your realization be:

God and I are one. All that the Father has
is mine. God has manifested Its life as my life;
God has manifested Itself as the *I* of my being and
has planted in the midst of it my infinity,
my abundance, my allness, my immortality,
my eternality. By reason of the grace
of God, this is true about everyone
on the face of the globe.

All Men Are Brothers

In order to make the life of God as the life of individual being demonstrable in your experience, you must go the second step of realizing that since this is true of you, it is true of all men. There is neither Jew nor Greek; there is neither white nor black; there is neither Oriental nor Occidental, for we are all one in our spiritual identity. "Call no man your father upon the earth: for one is your Father which is in heaven."[6] That makes all of us brothers and sisters, members of one family, of one household.

This is the truth whether the men and women of the world know it or not. The Master says, "Ye shall know the truth, and the truth shall make you free."[7] Now watch how it operates. When you are in any group of people, without any sense of self-righteousness, of being holier, better, or more valuable to God than the others, realize that there is but one Father, and you are all brethren. There are no barriers in that relationship, and then you can look upon any other person without judgment, criticism, or condemnation. Even if you are aware of sin, it would be with forgiveness. And what would happen to the other person? Would he not feel your lack of judgment? When a person sets himself up as better, holier, more righteous, more moral, or more honest than you, then a barrier would go up within you of defense, protecting yourself from whoever it is that is sitting in judgment on you.

If a person in any walk of life has designs on you, on your money, or in any way looks to you for something that is certainly not his right or due, that sets up a mental wall in you, and you automatically begin to protect yourself. The best illustration that I can give is that a person who has been trained to be a buyer of any kind of merchandise can practically smell a salesman coming along and up goes that wall of defense, with the immediate response, "No, I don't need anything." It is an automatic response, even if in the next minute that buyer may say, "Well, maybe."

You know how you feel if there is someone coming towards you who is about to ask you for money. You begin to formulate excuses before he gets to you. The same thing happens to animals when they sense cruelty or fear in a person. Automatically a wall of defense goes up, and they are on the offensive, which is their sense of self-protection.

The only way that you can love another is by looking upon him as an equal, without a trace of desire for anything from him. When you can do that, the person's guard goes down and you feel the love that is coming towards you and that you send back. Not recognizing what it is, he has the feeling, "Oh, here is a nice person," or "Here is a kind person." All he means is, "I can feel that he has no designs on me."

If you go into the business or professional world free of self-interest, without desiring, wanting, needing, begging, pleading for, or demanding anything, in the full consciousness that you and the Father are one and all that the Father has is yours, then you and your associates can meet as friends, and there is love between you. But let one trace of self-interest enter and watch how that bond of spiritual brotherhood is broken.

You Release Everyone From Any Obligation to You

There is no way in which you can refrain from desiring something that the other person has unless you know that you already have all of it, and there is nothing to desire. Ultimately you will go a step further in mystical consciousness and understand that since this is true of you and you already possess it all, you will reach that place in consciousness where you do not expect love, gratitude, appreciation, or co-operation from anyone. You are completely satisfied to have all of your needs met from within your own being. You release everyone in the world from any obligation to you, even the obligation of saying, "Thank you." Why? You get plenty of thanks from God, plenty of appreciation and gratitude. Whatever you do to or for anyone else, be sure you are not doing it for gratitude, appreciation, recognition, or reward. If you do otherwise, you are just entering into a merchandise bargaining. It is a trade, and a trade is not really love: it is a business deal.

Let Your Work Be Self-Fulfillment

What an individual does should be for the purpose of fulfilling and expressing himself. So if you would become a practitioner, do not think for a minute that you will reach your goal until you are honest enough to admit that you are doing the work to fulfill your own nature. That is the gift that has been given to you, and you must spend your talents. Unless you use your talents, they will rot away. Therefore, you are not working as a practitioner for the benefit of your patients, your students, or your world, but as a matter of your own self-fulfillment. Then you will never look to students or patients for appreciation, reward, or gratitude. You will know that your reward, gratitude, and your remuneration are in the deed.

This sets you very free. There may be quite a few patients or students who temporarily have no money, or enough merely for their own needs. And what are you going to do? Take some of that away from them, you who are supposed to have attained a consciousness that you have meat the world knows not of? You will have to acknowledge: "I am not doing this for money. I am not doing it for recognition or reward. This is the fulfillment of my own being, and whatever is necessary for my life will unfold from within my being." Then you will receive love, gratitude, reward, and compensation without limit.

It may not always come from the direction in which you are looking for it or expecting it, however. In fact you will not expect it from any direction but will let it come to you in accord with God's will. If someone is to provide it for you, it will be someone who at that moment can afford it without any loss or sacrifice to himself, and it may even be that your supply may not come from the person for whom you have done the most work.

If you are selling merchandise, it would be limiting God to look to this buyer or that buyer, this customer or that customer. But to present your product where it is right for it to be presented, with the idea that God governs the transaction, leaves the buyer perfectly free to say, "No", when he means no. It leaves him free not to have anything sold to him when he should not be buying, and it leaves you free to find your way to those who need what you have to offer. It operates through-out every phase of life.

Why Expressing Gratitude Tangibly Is Important

As you realize that you have "meat," you are not doing any-thing for compensation or reward: you are looking only to the source within yourself. That does not mean that you are entire-ly stupid. When you see a person violating what should be his sense of gratitude or recognition, you cannot help knowing the harm he is doing to himself. But you will never fall into the dan-gerous trap of believing he is withholding from you, because anyone who is withholding is withholding from himself. The bread he is casting on the water is the bread that is coming back to him and the bread he is not casting on the water is not com-ing back to him.

So you learn to live from the mystical basis of the full and complete realization that you are one with the Father and you have meat the world knows not of. You can perform every task that is given you to do without looking for praise, thanks, or for anything else. Then when these do come, you are appreciative of the fact that whoever is the instrument for your good is wide enough awake to be receptive and responsive to God, but you never lose sight of the truth that it is God functioning as that person's being. It is really your own self operating as the self of others. Your consciousness determines what comes back into your experience.

If I can sit here without judgment, criticism, or condemna-tion when I am teaching a class, without expecting anything of anyone, I can let truth pour through and students can feel a cor-responding sense of love because nobody is trying to take any-thing from them. They feel that confidence, assurance, and peace. And what do I bring to myself thereby? I bring to myself their love and friendship.

As long as I am performing my work without any sense of

doing it from the standpoint of duty or from the standpoint of "I owe it to you," or, "You owe it to me," as long as I do it from the sense of "I am fulfilling myself without seeking a return" once again that spiritual bond has come into the picture, that bond of invisible, spiritual love that has no material tie and looks to no one for anything.

As I walk out into the world of strangers in hotels or on the streets, conscious of the fact that God constitutes their individual being and realize God as the source, the soul, and the activity of every individual, I meet with co-operation all along the way. In other words, the oil of gladness, the oil of inspiration, the oil of love is the lubricant. That love has nothing to do with emotion. It has to do only with a recognition of true identity. Knowing that my neighbor is my self, and that my self is my neighbor, for we are one, of one household, one spiritual family, that God is their Father and mine is the only way I can really love my neighbor as myself. Then I bring back to me the reaction of co-operation, helpfulness, and whatever of a constructive nature may come up in the relationships of life.

Losing the Fear of Disease and Age

If I have the consciousness of God in the midst of me as being the only power and that power flowing out through me, I walk about with no fear of any external condition. I have no fear of germs I have no fear of accidents; I have no fear of persons I have no fear of animals, because there is no power external to me.

All power is given unto me. God has given me dominion by virtue of God's grace flowing through me. That is the only power unto any storm. The storm itself has no power. How can it have any power if I embody all power? And *I* is God. Then there is no power left for a storm. How can a germ have a destructive power if I embody all power?

As I walk through life realizing that the power of God is within me, flowing out to bless all who touch my consciousness, what I bring back to me is the power of God flowing through every creature on earth, whether it is human, animal, vegetable, or mineral. There are then no powers left outside to act upon me, and it is my own consciousness of truth that has brought this about.

Realizing that God is the only life, I understand that life is eternal, so I do not walk around fearing death. Once I have come to the place of not fearing death, the last enemy has been overcome. There are no others after that. Neither disease nor age can act except that it has death as its ultimate. Where there is no longer any fear of death, disease and age stop operating, because the ultimate of disease and age is death. What a person fears is not the age at which he is living, because he may be living beautifully this minute. He fears the future, which means death.

A person does not fear a disease. He fears the consequence of the disease, which ultimately is death. When the fear of death has been overcome through the realization that even death cannot separate him from the love of God, the life of God, and the consciousness of God, then neither age nor disease has any ground in which to flourish, none whatsoever. He becomes barren soil insofar as any seed of death, disease, or age is concerned.

God Appears As in a Moment of Need

Do you not see then that it is the activity of your consciousness that determines the reflex action that is your individual experience? As long as you are ignorant of the truth that would make you free, you are in bondage. It is not truth that will make you free: it is *knowing* the truth that will make you free. It is not God that will save you from anything: it is the *realization* of God. God is on every battlefield while men are being slaughtered. God is in every hospital where people are dying or wherever there is an accident. God is in the fire where people are being burned. And God does not stop these things and never will except as God is realized.

Many times the question is asked about persons, particularly fliers, who get into tough spots and then through turning to God find miracles take place that save them. Is it not clear that when there is not a sign or trace of human aid, they are forced to turn to God and in that moment of human helplessness they realize God? If they do not realize God they are not saved. When they do realize God, and in that desperate situation it is not difficult to realize God, they become aware of how close God is.

Charles Lindbergh, the Lone Eagle, tells how impossible it was for him to stay awake on that first trans-Atlantic flight. Many times he fell asleep, and when he awakened he knew that he was far off course, but he did not know how far, because he did not know how long he had slept, what his speed had been, or what the wind velocity was. He knew that in order to land where he planned to land, he would have to set himself back on course. When he left New York his computation showed him a certain place in Europe where he would land, somewhere between fifty and five hundred miles away from a particular spot, but it did not make any difference because he could quickly travel that distance and reach his destination. Yet there he was falling asleep and going off course and not knowing whether he was to the right or left, up or down.

Lindbergh later said that there was a man in the back of his airplane who told him what adjustments to make in his gadgets up front. He followed instructions and landed less than fifty miles away, almost on the spot where he was due, and then flew right into Paris, all because there was a man inside in the back of the plane who told him just what adjustments and calculations to make. And these calculations were correct. That is how close God is. But there has to be an innate something in those seeking guidance, which is a conviction of the transcendental.

There must be an inner conviction that there is something in them greater than themselves.

As long as you realize or give acknowledgment to the truth that there is a He within you greater than the world, a He that perfects that which concerns you, then this He can take over. It can even appear as a man in the back of the plane, who was not there when Lindbergh landed. You might say that his consciousness of the Presence brought about his safe journey across the sea, without which he would have gone down, not knowing where he was, or how.

The Activity of Truth in Consciousness Becomes the Substance of Your Experience

It is your consciousness that determines your experience. If your consciousness knows the truth that you are not a mortal who was conceived in sin and brought forth in iniquity, but that the I of you is the son of God, joint-heir to all the Father has, and you embody that in your consciousness and do not look out here, your consciousness of the infinite nature of God and the omnipresence of God produces the effect of harmony or abundance in your affairs.

If you look out and recognize God as individual being and if you see error and can forgive it on the ground of ignorance, and certainly not judge or condemn it, that person is bound to act with love and friendship toward you. You have ensured it. You have not left it up to his human nature or to his environment, and you have not left yourself at the mercy of other people's bias, bigotry, and hatred. You have taken the sting out of them because you have recognized their Christhood and in their Christhood there are no such qualities. To live free of the world's hatred, bias, and bigotry, it is necessary to live in the realization of its Christhood.

You will continue to meet persons who are so adamant in their mortality that this recognition does not change or influence them. There remains one further step, however. Regardless of what evil is aimed in your direction, do not personalize it. Realize: Thou hast not done this unto me, but unto God. Then let God take care of it in God's own way. But when you say, "Thou hast not done it unto me," do not pin it onto any person. Do not personalize it. The "thou" that you are talking about is the carnal mind. "Thou, carnal mind, that is acting in this way, you are not acting this way to me, but unto God." Then drop it. Impersonalize it at the other end and impersonalize it at this end, and there are no more persons involved.

One of two things happens when you turn the situation over to God: the persons involved either get healed or removed. If they remain adamant like our friends Ananias and Sapphira, they drop dead.[8] But if they are not quite that unyielding, they can be healed. I have witnessed indifference and outright antagonism dissolve when there was no personalization, no putting the blame on a person, but the realization: "This is not a man. There always has been the anti-Christ, and there always will be, not through hatred, but through ignorance. And so, Father, forgive them; they know not what they do."

Every moment determines what comes back into your experience by the truth or the lack of truth that is kept operative in your consciousness. If you walk without truth, just thinking worldly thoughts, then you are under the law and you have to accept a portion of good and evil. You have to pay the penalty of ignorance. When you walk with truth active in your consciousness, you are abiding in the Word and letting the Word abide in you. But be sure you know what the truth is. The answer always is, "I am. . . the truth."[9] If you ever get away from that and have an "I" *and* truth, you have duality again, twoness, and you bring duality back into your experience.

When you realize that you are not searching for truth or seeking truth, because the *I* you are is the embodiment of truth, then as you have a healing contemplative meditation, you do not have to worry about what truth to know about any person.

All you have to do is to turn within. Since you are the embodiment of truth, let this truth announce itself to you. It will come to you from the depth of the infinite storehouse of truth within yourself. It doesn't make any difference whether a person studies truth or not. The truth is all there, because God-consciousness is individual consciousness, and all that is in God is in everyone.

Many students erroneously believe that they do not have sufficient experience to do healing work. That is not true because if they have the ability to sit down and turn to the Father within and say, "You have given me all of the truth that You have. Now let me consciously know it," all the truth they need for their work, whatever it may be, will come to them, because it is not separate and apart from them.

The Freedom of I Am-ness

Truth is not in my books; truth is not in the Bible: truth is within you. Reading Infinite Way books or the Bible is just like priming a pump in order to make the water come up. So students can take Infinite Way books and the Bible and prime their consciousness. That is what they do, after which they sit back with: "Now it's Your turn, Father. Reveal to me the truth that is already embodied within me." Truth then can reveal itself, not the truth about the truth, but the truth which they are, the truth which they embody.

Your truth from now until eternity is embodied in the *I That I Am*, and *I Am* that truth. *I Am* is your supply, your bread, your meat, your wine, your water, your housing, your transportation, your immortality, and your eternality, all these embodied in that infinite storehouse which *I Am*.

Whatever knowledge you need is within you, just as it is within me. When I am in the midst of classwork every night, all the words and principles necessary for the work flow freely. But when I am not teaching a class, these words do not even deign to come to me. They stay locked up inside. If I am answering my mail and there is a need to write to a student or patient, or if I have to do an article, they come out again. But the minute I do not need them, they stay bottled up. If I sit down with a pen, the ink begins to leak. And fortunately it leaks words! Yes, all these messages are inside the pen. All they need is someone to push it. And the reason is found in the word *I*. *I* have meat the world knows not of, and that meat is in the form of everything necessary for my experience, not merely from the cradle to the grave, but on into infinity. The promise is, "I am with you alway, even to the end of the world."[10] So there can be no lessening of that *I* whether at the age of seventy, eighty, or ninety. It makes no difference—unless a person really wants to make the transition.

> *I* am the same yesterday, today, and forever. *I* never
> change. *I* am infinite. *I* am life eternal.

The whole secret of life is embodied in the *I* that you are, and your consciousness is the determining factor of what transpires in your life after you know this truth. Before you knew this truth, you were a victim of what others thought, what the universal belief may have been, whether the world was going through a period of those "good old days," whether it was a period of peace, of a war period, or of a cold war. Always you were the victim of what was going on, but now no more.

> "I and my Father are one,"[11] and the infinity of God is
> the infinity of my individual being. Now I know that
> I must open out a way. I must find a way to give, to
> share, to do, to be, and never sit and wait for
> something to happen to me. Always it is happening
> out from me. I embody, I embrace, and I include
> within myself the allness of God, and that allness flows
> by my sharing it. The more I share, the more I have.

ACROSS THE DESK

Today there is so much preoccupation with mind and mind control on the part of many persons that Infinite Way students need to be ever alert to its implications.

Mind is an instrument. Like all instruments, it can be used for good purposes or for evil purposes, depending upon the predilection of the one using it. If his mind is stronger than the mind of the person toward whom he is directing his mental activity, he may succeed in accomplishing his purpose, whether good or evil, unless his target, through spiritual awareness of the non-power of mind, does not yield himself to such activity.

Never give your mind over to be controlled by another person, but neither need you ever fear a person's misguided attempt to use mental power. To the spiritually awake, so-called mental power fades in the realization that God alone is power. Spirit is the only power, and that spiritual power cannot be used or directed. We can, however, open ourselves to let spiritual power flow through us as instruments for the pure activity of God, Spirit.

The meditation in chapter 10 of *The 1958 Infinite Way Letters* should prove very helpful to students in daily assuming dominion over the mind and becoming invulnerable to any form of mental activity.

Chapter Ten

The Invisible

Contemplative meditation can be a starting point for all meditation and can make it possible for a person to ease into a deeper form of meditation. That does not mean that there are not some persons already sufficiently adept in the art of meditation so that they no longer have to use the contemplative form as a first step. But these persons are few and far between. Unless you are among those in that category, it is wise to read the Bible or a spiritual or inspirational book for a few minutes until some particular idea or principle becomes uppermost in your mind. Then put the book aside and begin a contemplative meditation in which in all likelihood you will contemplate some truth that has struck you through what you have read.

It might be a scriptural passage such as: "Where the spirit of the Lord is, there is liberty."[1] Now contemplate that for a moment:

> "Where the spirit of the Lord is, there is liberty."
> Where is the spirit of the Lord? Is It not where I am?
> If I mounted up to heaven, would I not find the spirit of the Lord there? If I made my bed in hell, would
> I not find the spirit of the Lord there?

If "I walk through the valley of the shadow of
death,"[2] there, too, I will find the spirit of the
Lord, for the Lord is where I am, and the Lord,
the presence of God, fills all space. It fills this
space where I am. And even more important
than that is the truth that "the kingdom of
God is within"[3] me, so the presence of God
is within me. Yes, the presence of God,
closer than breathing, is within me.
The spirit of God is within me.

Here where I am, the spirit of the Lord is, and
"where the spirit of the Lord is, there is liberty."
So right here where I am, there is liberty.
I cannot be bound; I cannot be limited,
I cannot be circumscribed, for where God is,
I am. And where God is, there is liberty;
there is freedom, peace, and fulfillment.

In the presence of God is fulfillment, and that
presence is where I am. Therefore, here where
I am is fulfillment. I need not go to holy mountains,
to holy temples, or to holy men. Here where
I am is the presence of the Lord. And where
the presence of the Lord is, there is my freedom,
my joy, my peace, my abundance. If I do not
find it here where I am, I will not find it.
But I can find the spirit of the Lord only where
I am, omnipresence, all presence, the
presence of God where I am.

Usually by this time you have so thoroughly contemplated
the idea of omnipresence and of the spirit of the Lord where you
are that you can settle down into a peace in which for perhaps

ten, twenty, or thirty seconds you do not think at all. You are there in stillness with your ears open as if you were saying, "Speak, Lord; I am listening for Your voice." It may be only five, ten, or twenty seconds of a complete silence or stillness, but for that moment your meditation is complete. You can now feel that you have opened yourself to the presence of God; you have contemplated the Presence; you have realized It, and now you can go on and do whatever it is you have to do.

Consciously Place Your Loved Ones in God's Care

As a parent or grandparent, you are responsible for your children or your children's children, and it is natural that you should want to place them in God's care. Without a conscious awareness that they are in the Presence, they are not in God's care. If all children were in God's care, there would be no kidnappings or atrocities. So, while God is present everywhere, unless there is the conscious realization of this truth, all children are not in God's care.

Paul pointed that out when he said: "For they that are after the flesh do mind the things of the flesh. . .[and are] not subject to the law of God, neither indeed can be."[4] But if the spirit of God dwells in you, then you come under the law of God. Knowing this, you now wish to bring your child, or those for whom you are responsible, into and under the care and love of God. So you sit down for a contemplative meditation which is to be followed by that few seconds or a minute of waiting for God to place the seal on your meditation:

> "Whither shall I flee from thy presence?"[5]
> Whither shall my child flee from Thy presence?
> Thy presence fills all space;
> Thy kingdom
> is within the very consciousness
> of my child.

My child is the abiding place of God. His mind is
the temple of God; his body is the temple of God;
and God is in His dwelling place. Whithersoever
my child goes, the Lord has promised,
"I will never leave thee, nor forsake thee."[6]
Wherever my child goes, the Lord says, "I am with
you. I will be with you until the end of the world."

The spirit of the Lord God dwells in all children;
the spirit of the Lord God is the very breath
and the very life of their being and body,
the very intelligence of their mind.

God envelops them for God is in them,
and they are in God. In Thy presence is
fullness of life, and these children are
in the presence of God, for God is in them.
They are in God, and wherever they go
"the place whereon [they stand] is holy ground"[7]—
in the home, in the garden, out on the street,
out on the road, or in school. They cannot stray
from the loving arms of their Father, for God
is their Father. God it is who gave us these
children, and God is the ever loving, ever
protective Father. "Underneath are
the everlasting arms."[8]

After you have contemplated the principle of oneness, and
can say, "Speak, Lord; for thy servant heareth,"[9] wait in silence.
Soon you will feel a deep breath, a release, or a feeling that God
is on the scene, and you will know that your meditation for that
time is complete. You may even be led to speak directly to your
children at an appropriate moment:

"Children, wherever you are, you are in the kingdom of
God, for the kingdom of God is within you. Children, God is

your Father; hold His hand; feel His loving presence wherever you are. You and your heavenly Father are one, inseparable and indivisible; and you cannot stray from His presence, whether at home, at school, or at work.

"Children, consciously remember that God is your Father and that God walks with you and talks with you wherever you are. Just listen for the 'still small voice'[10] that is within you, and you will be guided, instructed, and protected.

"Remember, children, that God is also the Father of all whom you meet, whether they know it or not or whether the world calls them good or bad. You, children, must remember that God is their Father, their loving parent. They are never outside God's loving grace any more than you are, for we are all members of one household, all members of one family. God is in you, and you are in God; God is in your neighbor and your neighbor is in God, and we are all one."

A Contemplative Meditation Where a Physical Problem Is Involved

With your next meditation, you may have some form of illness to take up for somebody, and again you read for a while. If you are reading Infinite Way writings, you will probably very quickly come to some statement that will reassure you that there is but one power and that this condition could not exist if it were not for a universal belief in two powers. With that you put the book down and contemplate the subject of one power. Since God is that one power, you are back again to contemplating the subject of God:

God is infinite power,
but if God is infinite power is there any power in this
condition called sin or disease?
If God truly is omnipotent, all-power, is there any
power in an effect or a form?

God is the infinite formless; God is the infinite
invisible; and God is infinite power. All power is in
the Infinite Invisible, so there is no power in the
form, whether the form is called sickness, infection,
contagion, age, climate, or weather.

God is invisible, so all power must be invisible. If
God is infinite, power is not in the visible.

Invisible Life Acts Upon the Seed

Consider a seed that you are going to plant. Is there any
power in that seed? No, the seed will remain a seed forever
unless you put it back into its native element. When you place
it in the soil, something invisible begins to operate upon the
seed, in the seed, through the seed, and in the soil around the
seed. Soon that invisible something causes the seed to break
open and the life within the seed to sprout, to take root, and
eventually to work its way up through the ground.

Have you not seen how some plants can grow right up
through an inch of asphalt and break open the asphalt? Does the
plant do it or does the invisible power that was working through
the plant do it? If the plant did it, the plant would be smashed
and broken. If with your hand you tried to smash one inch of
asphalt, your hand would be smashed, so it cannot be the plant
but the invisible power that is operating in and through
the plant, and it goes before the plant to "make the crooked
places straight,"[11] to remove obstacles, to remove mountains, to
remove Red Seas.

Contemplating the Invisible Power of God

In your healing work when you are contemplating the
power of God, think of that power as an invisible power. Then
you will understand why there is no power in the visible form

or effect. It is the invisible power that flows through the form and through the effect to purify, cleanse, maintain, sustain, and to prepare a way for it to make the "crooked places straight," to provide many "mansions."[12]

As you contemplate the subject of one power from the standpoint of its invisibility, you will be surprised how quickly you lose the fear of persons, things, conditions, or circumstances. That is because you now have an inner conviction: All power is in the invisible; therefore, I need not fear what the mortal, material, or visible can do to me. Because all power is in the invisible, the Master could say to Pilate, that great temporal power, "Thou couldest have no power at all against me, except it were given thee from above."[13]

Having come to the end of that contemplative meditation on the subject of infinite all-power, again comes the attitude, "Speak, Lord; I am listening; I am receptive and responsive." Then just a few seconds—five, ten, twenty, or thirty seconds of silence, of inner peace which brings an assurance—and you are finished with that meditation.

A Meditation on Law

The next time you sit down to meditate with a problem on your mind, you may read something that has to do with law, so you will take law as the subject of your meditation:

Law, law – what do I know about law?
Well, the first thing I know is that God is the
lawgiver. God is the lawgiver? Yes, that is what
we are taught. That is what scripture tells us,
"The Lord is our lawgiver."[14] Is that true?
Who made the laws of mathematics?
Who made the laws of science?
Who made the laws of automotive engineering?
Who made the laws of television?

Did man make those laws or did he discover them?
Of course he discovered them.
They were already made.

Nobody invented the laws of wireless telegraphy
and the laws of navigation. Nobody created them:
they were discovered. But who made them?
They must have been here before man was on earth.
They have always existed in the mind of
God, and they existed as law: the laws of
mathematics, the laws of aerodynamics, the laws
of music, the laws of composition, the laws
of art, the laws of bridge building,
the laws of architecture.

God is the lawgiver. Since God is infinite and
made all the laws that exist, they must all be
made in the image and likeness of God.
God could not create anything destructive to
Himself or to His own creation. God is love
and God is wisdom; therefore, all laws that
exist are laws of wisdom and love.

What about these other laws: laws of disease,
laws of sin? They are not laws at all because
there cannot be God as the lawgiver and laws
of disease and death. Light and darkness
cannot occupy the same place, nor can life
and death or God and disease occupy the
same place. Whatever laws there are, are
laws of God, and they are laws of good.

Anything parading as law, anything counterfeiting
the law of God, anything believed to be law

which is not of God is not law
and does not have power.
Does a judge have power?
Does a jury have power? No, law alone has power
and that law is invisible and impersonal.

As you contemplate the subject of law, again you come to the end of your contemplation. You are receptive; your ears are open; and in a few moments comes that inner peace, that glow, that something that tells you that this meditation is complete.

No Subject Is Too Insignificant or Unimportant for Meditation

Whatever subject comes up in your life, whether the solution to some problem or a decision to be made, it must be the subject of meditation. If you are going out to buy a suit or a dress you really should not do it without meditation. Why? It is easy enough to buy clothing humanly, but it could turn out to be not quite the clothing you would find and buy or the price at which you would find it if you first meditated, not on buying clothing but on God as your wisdom, God as the love, God as your caretaker, God as that which provides for you. Then you would go out and find that God had literally provided for you much better and much more reasonably than your human wisdom could have done for you.

Anything that concerns your life is not too unimportant for meditation, because the more you practice meditation, the more you come to that place where you do not live by your own wisdom or your own power but where you live by Grace. You are not to expect some far-off God to sit around thinking about you or doing things for you, but rather you are to contemplate God. "Ye shall know the truth,"[15] and then this truth that you know is the truth that goes before you to break the one inch of asphalt, to prepare a place for you, to prepare mansions for you.

Living the Life of Meditation

Life becomes a going from one meditation to another until eventually the day comes when you are meditating without closing your eyes. You are meditating while driving your car, because you are inwardly contemplating the truth of being. No matter what you are doing, there is always some area of consciousness, some space in your mind, wherein you can contemplate reality even while doing the mundane things of life.

You may use scripture or passages from the Infinite Way writings to trigger your contemplative meditation. Then have your contemplative meditation and wait for the seal to be set upon it. As you become increasingly proficient in contemplative meditation, the silent meditation lasts longer. One day you will be very much surprised that while you may have thought that you had been meditating for three, four, or five seconds, sixty whole seconds have gone by. You had lost track of time, and only after a minute were you propelled back into the world of time and space.

As this becomes your mode of life, eventually after your contemplative meditation, you will be in meditation two, three, five, or ten minutes without for a second being aware of the fact that time is passing. You will be in that timeless, spaceless world which is the kingdom of God.

Living the Contemplative Life, You Become Less Vulnerable to Universal Claims

Even with increased meditation, problems do come to you. There is a universal claim of a selfhood apart from God, of a law apart from God, of a health and of a power apart from God, and this belief is always operating. If people are sick, however, it is not because of any fault of theirs. It is not because of any sins of omission or commission, except the sin of not knowing the truth, the sin of ignorance. The human race is ignorant, and that is why the human race suffers sin, disease, and accident.

In proportion as you live this life of contemplative meditation in which you are acknowledging God as the only power, God as the only being, with your mind constantly resting in the assurance that all power is in the invisible and not in the visible, gradually you are not quite so subject to disease. Illness then may be only an occasional experience, and when it is, it is neither your fault nor mine. It is the heavy pressure of universal belief.

Frequently these claims hit on days when the world news is most upsetting, on days when there is fear of a bomb, a flu epidemic, or a polio epidemic. Those are the days when you are the most subject to the ills of the flesh and it is those days when you need to be even more alert in your realization that there is no power in the visible universe: in man, in weather, in infection or contagion, or in whatnot, for God is the only power, and God is invisible. Therefore, all power is in the invisible. As you pray without ceasing, which means, knowing the truth without ceasing, the truth that you know keeps you free.

Knowing There Is No Power in Form or Effect Eliminates Fear

If you will always remember to impersonalize and never blame yourself, your patient, or your student for his ills, you will have half the victory won. The other half comes with the realization that one power actually means no power: no power in any form or effect. Is there a fever? Let there be a fever, for there is no power in form or effect. Do not fight it; do not argue with it; do not try to get rid of it. Recognize the truth that all power is in the invisible governing visible form and effect. Then you can sit beside your patient who has a fever, and rest in the assurance, "I in the midst of thee, the invisible power, is the only power, and that which is visible is not power."

Soldiers in combat have said that they never fear the bullet they can hear, because it has already gone by. Why then should you fear the condition that you can see, hear, taste, touch, or smell since it has already gone by? The power itself is in the invisible. Try it and see how you lose your fear. Once your fear of any person or condition is lost, it has no hold over you whatsoever.

When physical exhaustion is present, the best thing to do is not to fight it but to lie down or sit down and "agree with thine adversary"[16]:

> Let me be still and wait for it to pass.
> Certainly there is no power in it.
> God never made an absence of God,
> and all that exhaustion can be is an
> absence of God. In the presence of
> God there is enough strength to break
> open one inch of asphalt. God never
> made an absence of Himself, so God
> never made exhaustion, and I can wait
> for this belief to pass by, and if
> I do not fight it, it will pass.

Illumination Reveals the Omnipresence of Supply

Never dwell on the forms supply is to take, whether a house, sufficient money for your needs, or for little luxuries or entertainment. That would be a sin. If you really want to commit a sin take thought for "what ye shall eat, or what ye shall drink."[17]

Under no circumstances are you ever to be tempted to take thought for things. Your meditation is for the contemplation and the realization of God. When you have attained the realization of God, all things are added unto you. In every area where there appears to be a lack of supply, turn to God for enlightenment. If more oil is needed, be assured God quickly reveals where it is to be found, how to produce it, or where to find a substitute for it. God has not created you to leave you hanging in space; God has not created you to let you lack for food.

When you turn to the Father within, you will learn a great secret about God. God did not create you and then leave you without food, clothing, or housing, or whatever it is that is necessary for your experience. Never fear shortages. Always go to the Father within and do not pray for what the world prays for. Pray only for God's grace, or the light which God can give you, the illumination of His plan, and you will find that as soon as oil runs out, and I am sure it will, you will have nuclear energy or some other form of power. So it will be with everything. There is no provision in the kingdom of God for the destruction of God's kingdom.

Nonexistence
Cannot Be Explained

There is a transcendental consciousness, a consciousness beyond your human mind. There is no spiritual power in your human mind. There is no spiritual power in what you know or what you learn. Spiritual power is embraced in something which is called "that mind which was also in Christ Jesus,"[18] transcendental consciousness. In India it is called the Buddha-mind and in Japan *satori*. When once the state of *satori,* the state of Buddha-mind, or the Christ-mind is attained, there are not two powers operating.

As a human being, you entertain what is called a human sense of mind, which is composed of two powers. The origin for it is revealed in the second chapter of Genesis which explains that the acceptance of the belief in two powers brought about the human mind with its woes. How it could have come about when there is a transcendental mind which really is infinite can be explained only on the basis that in and

172 of spiritual Living

within the scope of the transcendental mind there is but one power and whatever exists outside of that scope exists only as *maya* or illusory sense. It actually has no existence and, having no existence, cannot be explained.

The nonexistent city that you sometimes see out in the desert cannot be explained, for it has no existence, or the nonexistent body of water that is sometimes seen out in the desert cannot be explained, for it has no existence. So it is that what is called this earthly existence that has birth and death is the product of an illusory sense that has no existence and for that reason cannot be explained.

It is possible for an individual to believe that two times two is five even though there is no such thing in existence as two times two is five, never has been, and never could be. As a matter of fact, there never was a flat world; there never was a square world. Yet you can see how in our ignorance we could accept appearances through illusory sense and behold that which never existed. Now try to explain what happened to that square world or to that flat world.

I cannot personally explain the nonexistent. I do not know how to explain that which I have seen has no existence, but there is a transcendental state of consciousness which is something beyond your thinking, reasoning mind, and it is this that is your salvation on the mystical path. This transcendental consciousness is your consciousness which is something beyond your thinking, reasoning mind, and it is this that is your salvation on the mystical path. This transcendental consciousness is your consciousness in proportion as you learn the nature of invisible law, invisible power, invisible presence, invisible life, invisible being, and furthermore learn that this visible world is only the outer form or expression and that it is animated and impelled by the invisible just as the invisible begins to work through the seed in the ground and begins to send up shoots that break through an inch of asphalt. It is a mystery; it is a miracle; but it is truth.

ACROSS THE DESK

Parents are often concerned about the academic attainment or social adjustment of their children. There is no better time than early in the school year to translate this concern into action, rather than to experience the rude awakening that frequently comes at the end of the school term.

Students of a spiritual way of life sometimes forget to provide the simple but important help they can give their children by creating a quiet and peaceful environment in which there is a minimum of extraneous distraction in the form of family conflict or the continuous blasting of a television set. Furthermore, a balanced program can be set up, providing adequate time for play but also a regular time and place for study, and a wise discipline that demands from each his best.

In addition to the right physical environment, and far more important, parents and grandparents can have daily meditations for their offspring in which the children are consciously released to the fulfillment of the *I* within them through a realization of their spiritual identity, thereby helping to establish and maintain them in their eternal relationship of oneness with their source. You will find an example of how to do this in this month's *Letter*. In the realization of that oneness, the intelligence, wisdom, love, and infinite capacity of the Father are revealed as the qualities of the son. To give children wise parental guidance and to enfold them in the parents' realized consciousness of truth is real love, a love which is always coupled with wisdom.

TAPE RECORDED REFERENCES
Prepared by the Editor

"Law"

"Your conscious communion with God lifts you into a state of consciousness where materiality does not reign, where there are no laws of matter. Did you ever stop to realize that any heal-ing you have ever experienced of your own or another's has been a proof that there are no laws of matter? There is no such thing as a violation of a law or the setting aside of a law. . . .Every heal-ing is a proof that there is no such thing as a law of matter. . . .

"Every time you behold some form of deformity, sin, dis-ease, or error, consciousness must be alert: There are no laws of matter. Laws of matter are not laws but beliefs, and they are not power. God is the only power. That must be done consciously twenty, thirty, fifty times a day. . . . Twenty-four hours a day refute every appearance of a law of matter until it becomes so imbued in consciousness that just walking down the street dis-pels these erroneous appearances."

Joel S. Goldsmith, "There Is No Law of Matter or Disease," *The 1953 Los Angeles Practitioners' Class.*

"On the spiritual path you ignore evil humanity and you ignore good humanity: you go down the middle path of realiz-ing spiritual identity. . . .With almost every claim that comes to an individual there is a sense of law—some material law, some mental law, some moral law, some legal law—but you ignore these and go right down the middle path of spiritual law. You do not try to change bad material law into good material law. You do not try to nullify a mental law or establish one. . . . If God is spirit and God is the law-giver, then all law is spiritual. The laws of infection or contagion, or the law of karma. . . only exist and operate in what is called 'this world.' . . .

"As long as we have reliance on material modes and means of living, we are under the necessity of making a transition to spiritual dependence. If we have too much belief in medical laws, health laws, economic laws, we must be prepared to make the transition from the universal belief in these laws to the recognition of spiritual law as the only law. . . . There must be a gradual transition that takes place through a daily communion with truth, through a daily period of meditation in which we ponder the spiritual law of health one day, the spiritual law of life another day, and the spiritual law of relationships another day. . . .

> There are no laws out here acting upon me
> for good or for evil. Why? Because I am life eternal;
> I am the law; I—that part of me which is God,
> the kingdom of God within me—is the source
> of life, the source of law, the source of supply,
> the source of health, and therefore it never
> comes to me: it flows out from me."

Joel S. Goldsmith, "The Middle Path,"
The Second 1960 London Closed Class.

Chapter Eleven

Impersonalizing the Visible

It may seem difficult for the student to impersonalize evil, but the impersonalizing of good is even more difficult. In impersonalizing good we have to realize that whatever of good is flowing out through us is not really of us but of God. We are the instruments, the transparencies, the vehicles through which, and as which, God functions. The Master said:

> Why callest thou me good? there is none
> good but one, that is, God
> Matthew 19:17

> My doctrine is not mine, but his that sent me.
> John 7:16

> If I bear witness of myself, my witness is not true.
> John 5:31

If our philanthropies consist in making contributions to worthy causes, we cannot claim to be philanthropic, benevolent, or good. Rather we must understand that we are instruments through which God, good, flows out in the direction of different philanthropies. If we are honest or moral, we do not say that we are honest or moral. These are qualities of God, and we are but the instruments or transparencies through which these qualities appear on earth.

Impersonalize Wisdom and Intelligence

There are those who are unusually intelligent in many ways, have high IQ's, or are more intelligent in even higher ways than that, having a wisdom which an IQ does not always indicate. An individual should realize that whatever of intelligence or wisdom is manifesting through him or his experience is really the wisdom of God, and he is the instrument through which it appears or as which God functions. Because it is God's wisdom expressing through him, it is infinite.

In thus impersonalizing good by not claiming it as of ourselves, we open ourselves to an infinite capacity to express good, an infinite capacity to express intelligence, wisdom, love, and life. The moment we claim anything for ourselves, we are necessarily limiting whatever it is we are claiming. When we acknowledge that we can of our own selves do nothing, we then make room for infinite good to be expressed through and as us.

If we understand that all wisdom belongs to God, that it is infinite, and then open ourselves to its activity, we have a far greater capacity for learning, understanding, and expressing than we ever could have of our human selfhood.

Be an Instrument Through Which God Performs His Functions

There are occasions when it would be hypocrisy to say that we are able to forgive. There are some offenses we cannot forgive; we cannot forgive the damage some people have done. The hurt and harm they have done, whether to individuals or to nations, is so great that we would find it impossible of ourselves to be forgiving. Even if we could pay lip service and say that we forgive, in our hearts we know that it is not completely so. But again we have recourse to: "I can of mine own self do nothing."[1] I cannot forgive this experience, this person, or this event, but certainly I can pray that God forgive him. Even if I humanly do not have that capacity for forgiveness, at least I know enough to know that forgiveness is right and, therefore, let me pray:

> Father, forgive him, that he be not held
> in bondage to his offenses but that he
> be forgiven and that the spirit of Christ
> open his consciousness to truth, to
> reality, to the right.

By impersonalizing good in every way, we make ourselves instruments or transparencies through which God can perform His functions. Once we have attained, even in a small measure, the ability to impersonalize good insofar as it concerns us, we then turn our attention to the world, to our family, community, and friends, and begin to realize that they also are transparencies for God, that they of themselves can be neither good nor evil, that they of themselves can neither give nor withhold, that they of themselves are not power but are transparencies for God.

Regardless of what human circumstance or conditions may be touching me as I teach a class, you are not to look to me for spiritual instruction but to God. Knowing that I am but the transparency, nothing would happen to the truth. In a very short time another transparency would arise. If for any reason I should retire from active work, except for that momentary flutter that we all feel at leaving one another, it should not disturb anyone, knowing that this message is of God and that at best I have been but the transparency for it. God has billions of transparencies to raise up to perform His work. The work will go on just the same because the same God will be sending it forth into expression by means of another transparency.

Every bit of truth that has ever come to earth has come through an individual consciousness. But when Lao-tze, Buddha, Moses, Elijah, Isaiah, Jesus, John, and Paul left the scene, that did not stop truth. In every age or whenever needed, another transparency appeared through which God could function so that His message could reach consciousness.

Invisible Grace Restores the Years of the Locust

When you think about your employment, you should never fear its loss, because whether it is your business, your profession, or your job, it is but an instrument, a vehicle; it is not God. It is an instrument through which God's grace is reaching you. If the temple or the body of your business, your fortune, or your profession were destroyed, in three days the same grace of God that gave it to you would raise up another for you, unless you had become so hypnotized that you just sat looking at it and mourning. If you could quickly awaken and see that if the body of your business, profession, or job were destroyed, and that in three days it would be raised up again, you would never fear loss.

When you impersonalize, you will never be brought to a state of fear because, regardless of what is destroyed in the physical universe, the same principle that produced it will immediately begin producing another one.

The city of Hiroshima, which was blasted completely off the earth in 1945, today is more magnificent and more populous than ever. The only reminder of that holocaust is the memory and perhaps the fact that it looks a little too new to be natural.

Regardless of what fate overtakes the world, the same principle that brought forth what is destroyed would begin the very next moment reproducing it until in a brief time there would not even be scars left. It is the invisible that is the real; it is the invisible that is the creative principle; it is the invisible and impersonal which produces and reproduces.

If you strip your trees of all their fruit this year, next year they will have more fruit. Whether you eat the fruit, give it away, sell it, or it is blown away by the wind, next year your trees will bear again because in due time the invisible spirit of life will show forth that which is eternally in operation.

It has been said that no board of directors ever brought through anything worthwhile. If you investigate that I think you will find it is true. Everything worthwhile that has ever come to this earth has come through individual consciousness, whether it was the message of great spiritual teachers or whether it was the wireless telegraphy of Marconi or the great work of Einstein. Regardless of the nature of the good, it has come forth through the consciousness of an individual.

All works are of God, but all works come through the instrumentality of an individual. Therefore if you can realize that you are on the first rung of the ladder of impersonalization and also on the first rung of the ladder of losing your fears, realizing that your good comes not from man but *through* man, that there is an infinite invisible that is the source of all being, you immediately begin to lose your fear of what is in the world. You do not fear the loss of persons; you do not fear the loss of money; and you do not fear the loss of home or business. You understand that should any loss arise it is but a momentary experience of the day, but the principle which brought whatever appears to have been lost into existence continues to function, and in three days, less or more, the body, the temple, will be raised up again.

The Consciousness of Truth Is the Healer

When it comes to the healing work, it is important to remember that whereas God is the source of all good, it is the

degree of *realized individual consciousness* that determines
what degree of harmony, wholeness, and completeness will
come into your experience or mine. If you claim that God is
the healer, you must mean something different from what the
world understands, because looking around the world God is
not the healer. When you look into metaphysical or spiritual
healing, you will also find that if God were the healer, all
healers would do equal healing, because it would be the same
God doing it.

Regardless of what teaching you are following, whether the
Infinite Way or some other teaching, the teaching in and of
itself cannot guarantee you a healing. It is the degree of realized
consciousness of the practitioner. The principles of the Infinite
Way are true and have been tried through many years of practice. The record is good. That which has not been proved has
not been included in the writings. So it is safe to say that as of
today there are no finer works on spiritual healing, no more
complete, no more tested or tried, than these. If the principles
would heal you, the fact that they are in forty books and book-
lets would save the world. But that is not true.

Only in the degree that the consciousness of what is in those
books is attained do healing works come through. There maybe
some practitioners doing beautiful work and others using the
same writings doing less beautiful works, and still others doing
very little. The message is not responsible. The message is truth.
It is the degree of evolved consciousness that determines the
degree of healing brought forth.

Those who work the most faithfully, who devote and dedicate themselves to working with these specific principles will of
course in time attain the highest evolved consciousness. The
principles are true, but they require practice, devotion, and dedication. The most serious cases will not be healed in the beginning of our work, and sometimes we will not even heal the most
serious ones at the latter part of our work, unless we can devote
the necessary time and attention to these cases. There can be no

reliance on petitioning some supernatural power for help: God, heal my baby; God, do this for Mrs. Jones who deserves it because she is a good woman. There is no such thing as reliance on any kind of a supernatural happening. But there is a transcendental state of consciousness.

Unconditioned Mind

There is one mind. There is not a human mind and a Christ-mind. You do not get rid of one mind and get another mind, but as you abide in the principle of God, the invisible, as the only power, you lose your fear of other powers and at the same time you are coming into a state of consciousness devoid of fear. It is your same mind but now it is your mind devoid of fear, at least in some measure. The measure of your lack of fear determines the measure of your Christliness.

As you work with the subject of law, realizing that since God is the lawgiver there can be but one law and that spiritual, you begin to lose your fear of the laws of infection, contagion, accident, birth, and heredity. As you lose that fear, you have less of the human sense of mind and a greater degree of the Christly sense of mind.

By continuing to work with these specific principles, eventually you attain some degree of the unconditioned mind, and the unconditioned mind means that "mind which was also in Christ Jesus,"[2] a mind not conditioned to fear, a mind not conditioned with thoughts of limitation, and a mind that does not recognize birth or death as the two ends of man. The unconditioned mind does not react to the world of appearances but reacts only to the realm of truth.

No one has attained this unconditioned mind in its absolute sense. Even the Master in his final experience on earth showed that he was not wholly unconditioned when he asked the disciples to stay awake to pray with him and when he asked that the cup might pass from him. He was reacting in some measure to the world of appearances. Yet he had a high enough realization so that he could prove his conditioning to be only temporary and finally he could say: "Thy will be done."[3] Through the unconditioned mind, he was looking only to the realm of the real to act as a power in his experience.

Progress is individual, and the depth of our demonstration is individual. The degree of work we put into our search for God determines the degree of unconditioned mind we will achieve. The Master showed us how difficult the way is, and all of us will discover that there are difficulties in every step of the way. Whether or not we shall completely surmount those while on this plane I would not know. I only know that no one I know of has ever made the supreme demonstration of complete Christliness. It is possible, however, for each one of us to go far on the spiritual path and to be able to show forth the fruits of the principles.

"Resist Not Evil"[4]

This brings us to another characteristic of the transcendental consciousness of "that mind which was also in Christ Jesus." That is Jesus' teaching of nonresistance. The disciples thought they had power over the devil through the name of Jesus, but he assured them they had no such power: "Rejoice not, that the spirits are subject unto you; but rather rejoice, because your names are written in heaven,"[5] meaning rejoice only that you know that devils are not power. You know there is no force or power to be used over the evils of this world. You are not to take up the sword—the metal sword or the mental sword—for you are not to resist evil.

Another attribute of "that mind which was also in Christ Jesus," the transcendental consciousness, is the degree in which you do not refute, deny, fight, or try to overcome the evils of this world; but rather "resist not evil," or as Paul said: "None of these things move me."[6] This sometimes gives a sense of inner peace and power. "None of these things move me," for I know that in the omnipotence of God, there is no other power. Therefore I can be like Hezekiah who said, "With him is an arm of flesh."[7] Then his people rested in his word and watched the enemy destroy itself.

God's Creation
Embodies No Discord or Evil

In the healing work, as you attain an inner stillness, not trying to remove some person's fever, cold, or cough but sitting in an assurance of God's presence, conscious that God fills all space, that "the kingdom of God is within you,"[8] and *I* within you is God, in that receptive attitude, you can receive an impulsion from God within you. You experience a weight dropping from the shoulder, and receive a sense of release, an inner smile, an awareness that God is on the scene.

Instead of shouting out that somebody was healed, inwardly glorify God because it has been revealed that disease is not a reality, not a power, not a person, and that disease has no law, no life, and no truth. Disease was never ordained by God; it was never created by God. Therefore it has no reality. If disease had ever been created by God, Jesus would be one of the great sinners because in his ministry he went about removing disease. What a sin it would be to remove God's creation! But disease is not a part of God's creation. Otherwise Jesus would not have been ordained to prove its nothingness.

The mission of the Master was to prove that God has no pleasure in your dying, that death is an enemy to be overcome. Neither death, disease, nor old age is visited upon you by God. These have come upon persons in their ignorance of God, but wherever God is known aright there is life eternal. To understand God as the creative principle of life you have to go even further and realize that since life is infinite, there is no room for death.

Limitation Is
No Part of God's Creation

To know God as "the health of [your] countenance"[9] means to know God as infinite. In infinite health there is no room for sickness. To understand God aright is to understand God as the creator of all the wealth of which you are cognizant here on earth: the wealth of trees, grass, flowers, and fruit, the wealth of diamonds, gold, silver, pearls, coal, and uranium. Since this wealth is infinite there is no room for lack or limitation, which cannot exist in the world of God's creating. They exist only in a conditioned mind that limits God.

If your mind is conditioned to limit God, that limitation becomes a part of your experience, but the moment you bring about an unconditioning of your mind you begin to show forth the infinite riches of God. Since "God is no respecter of persons"[10] those riches belong as much to you as to anyone else on the face of the earth.

The mistake is in trying to get this wealth away from somebody else instead of realizing, "the earth is the Lord's, and the fulness thereof"[11] and "Son. . . all that I have is thine."[12] Why is there an abundance of grass, an abundance of trees, fruit, pearls, diamonds, and coal, an infinity of salt in the sea? It was not sent here for you or for me. It was sent here to glorify God, and it belongs to you and to me, but not to be able to divide it. God's grace cannot be divided. It is infinite, and it is infinite in the experience of all who open their consciousness to God's infinity.

The Impersonal
Nature of God's Grace

Personalizing wealth and believing you have a great deal of it or a little of it is enough to destroy it. Rather impersonalize wealth in this realization:

"The earth is the Lord's and the fulness
thereof. . . . Son. . . all that I have is thine."
I will look only unto God for my grace
because His grace is my sufficiency
in all things.

In this meditation you are impersonalizing. This will seriously modify your concept of prayer, because now you cannot pray to God to have Him do something for Jones, Brown, or Smith. God is not functioning for Jones, Brown, or Smith: God is functioning for His own glory, and Jones, Brown, or Smith is going to receive help when the practitioner or the patient begins to realize that God's goodness was not sent to earth with anyone's name on it. God's goodness cannot be directed to any particular person.

Only in proportion as you are impersonal in your prayers, realizing that God's grace is bestowed on every individual, are you praying the "effectual fervent prayer of a righteous man."[13] If you try to claim it for yourself, you lose it; if you try to direct it into some particular channel for your benefit, you lose it. The minute you ask God to send something to you, you lose it. Instead, you must realize the impersonal and universal nature of God's grace, available to saint or to sinner, white or black, free or bond, Jew or Gentile, not meant for one race, nation, or religion.

God's grace is to glorify God, and that Grace can glorify God only in being made available universally everywhere to everyone. "A thousand may fall at thy side, and ten thousand at thy right hand,"[14] as long as the rest of the world does not open its consciousness to receive God's grace. So, too, as Jesus considered the obtuseness of Jerusalem, he said, "and ye would not."[15] Yes, God's grace is available to every person, but not every person will avail himself of it, just as your supply, health, home, and body may all prosper, and still the person nearest and dearest to you may be untouched.

If a person closes his mind to this infinite storehouse of good, preferring to get it from somebody rather than from the source, he shuts himself off. Do not you be a party to that shutting off by believing as he may believe, that it comes from someone other than the source. You maintain always that "the earth is the Lord's, and the fulness thereof," and that the Father has given it to every individual.

The Invisible Nature of Supply

If temporarily you are caught up in the mesmerism of a materialistic world, you might wonder how everyone can have all. Try then to remember that supply is not material: it is spiritual. It is of the same nature as integrity. Is it not possible for one individual to be a hundred per cent moral and yet there be enough morality left over so that every other person can also be a hundred per cent moral? Is it not possible to be completely honest, loving, and just and yet find that everybody else can also be completely loving, honest, and just?

The qualities of God are spiritual, and what we call supply is just as invisible as God. What appears to us visibly is not supply. What appears to us visibly is the *effect* of supply. If the apples on your tree were supply, the moment you ate them you would have no supply. But that is not true because as long as there is life in the tree more apples will appear. So you can spend your money wisely without undue concern, if you realize that it is not supply: it is the effect of supply. The supply itself is as invisible as the supply that puts apples on apple trees and roses on rosebushes.

In your prayers it is not necessary to pray that God do something for you or for Jones, Brown, or Smith. Let your prayer be the recognition and realization of invisible good, omnipresent and omnipotent. Let it be the realization that "the place whereon thou standest is holy ground,"[16] and that this *you* is the you of everybody everywhere. You may wonder how a particular individual will benefit by that kind of prayer. The answer is that he will benefit by it because he has brought himself to your consciousness.

Impersonal Prayer

If you are going to pray for your flower garden, you do not go around and ask each bush if it has a name, and you do not try to direct God to a particular bush, a particular tree, or a particular corner of your garden. That would be foolishness. But if you were to pray for your garden, you would have a contemplative meditation:

> Who is the author of all gardens?
> God. Who alone can make a tree? God.
> God is the invisible life, substance, activity,
> and law unto all form, including this and
> every other garden. God is in the midst of this
> garden. God is its nourishment, its food,
> its substance, and the law of this
> garden and all other gardens.
> God is the invisible life of all form.

Because you do have your garden in mind, your garden will respond to this truth more readily perhaps than the garden of your neighbor, who may be mentally shut up inside of a conditioned mind thinking in terms of me and mine.

As you are praying for the unity and harmony of your family, it will not be because you expect God to do something for your family that God is not doing for other families. But when you sit down to pray, you do have, and rightly so, your own family in your consciousness for God has given you the responsibility of this family and therefore you accept that responsibility and have a period of contemplation on the subject of family:

There is but one Father: God is the
father of this family. This household is
the household of God, and every individual
in this household is of the family of
God, all heirs of God and
"joint-heirs with Christ."[17]

The function of this family is to
show forth God's grace, God's presence,
God's beauty, God's strength, the harmony
of God's being, and the wealth
of the kingdom of God.

This is a spiritual family.
We are one in divine sonship, all children of God.

I and the Father are one; I and my family
are one; I and all families are one.
This is a universal truth, and it is the
truth about every family on the
face of the globe.

Your family will in all likelihood respond to this meditation
more than some others because your family is embraced in your
consciousness. Your family is looking to you to maintain a consciousness of truth until it can maintain its own.

When you are asked for help from a patient, God is not
going to do anything for that patient. God's work is already
done. You are the one who is going to know the truth that is to
make him free, and the truth you are to know is:

God is omnipotent, omnipresent,
and omniscient.
God is the substance of all form;
God is the only law, the only activity,

the only being, the only presence.
All that God is, I am.
All that God is, you are.
All that God is, he is, she is, and it is.
We are of the household of God,
the one infinite family,
universally children of
God, heirs of God to all the immortality,
eternality, and infinity of God.

Why a Particular Person Benefits From Impersonal Prayer

The patient who has asked for help will benefit more than other persons in the world, because this particular patient has brought himself to your consciousness or you have brought him to your consciousness, and he is held in it. Prayer then becomes impersonalization, a realization of the infinite universal nature of God and of God's grace equally throughout this universe. You will thus be loving your neighbor as yourself, but you will bring the greatest blessing to those who have brought themselves within range of your consciousness. They will benefit, not because God is going to do something special for them or because God is going to do something special for you or through you: they will benefit because you are knowing God aright, knowing God as the infinite, eternal, immortal life of all being. You are knowing God as the spiritual law, the spiritual activity of all creation.

The person who has brought himself to your consciousness will receive more benefit than the thousand here and the ten thousand there who are content to remain entombed within their own mind, thinking of themselves as something special, something extraordinary, or something that God ought to listen to, God ought to benefit, or to whom God ought to give grace. God's grace is universal.

Impersonalizing Gratitude

You are not to be grateful for the forms of good that come into your individual experience, because that is personalizing it as if God were sending it just to you. Looking out into your garden, you are grateful that there is an invisible being that sends Itself forth as apples, roses, tulips, pineapples, or whatever, and not just for the things of themselves. You are grateful that there is a law of nature which sends forth trees, plants, blossoms, fruits, vegetables, animals, and minerals. It does not send these to you. It just sends them forth to glorify Itself. Therefore, be thankful that all of this good has been sent forth to this earth.

When you say grace at table, and in our particular family, grace is always done silently, never orally, it is not thankfulness for the food on our table. It is a thankfulness that God sends food into the world, that God's grace has filled this land with food and with all those things that provide food, make for food, and preserve food. It is not because you have something to eat that you are grateful. It is that food has been provided for mankind. That is what should evoke your gratitude. You are grateful that there is oil in the ground, not because you own any of it, but because it is there for the world, and as a part of the world naturally it is a part of your life and you are a part of it, but only because you are part of God's world.

Once you realize that your gratitude is for God expressing Himself in infinite forms and varieties of good and that all of this is available to mankind, you are really impersonalizing your gratitude. You are grateful, not for selfish little you. If there were no food on your table you should be grateful that there is food in the world, because there are four billion other people who are to be fed, and they would not be if there were no food. There would not be food if it were not for God's grace. So even if for some reason or other you have to miss some of life's good, still be grateful that "the earth is the Lord's, and the fulness thereof," and it belongs to all mankind.

ACROSS THE DESK

Just as the accent in the word "Thanksgiving" should be on "giving", so the accent in our lives should also be on giving. Thanksgiving serves as a reminder to us to pause to review our abundant blessings. In this pause we remember that giving is really an outpouring from the source within. The purpose of our being is not to acquire things to be thankful for, but to be instruments through which the blessings of God flow.

With such an awareness, our lives take on a freshness and joy of purpose. Every day becomes not only a day of thanksgiving, but of God giving and God living.

TAPE RECORDED EXCERPTS
Prepared by the Editor

"Receptivity as Related to Givingness"

"The question of receptivity comes up very often in this work: 'How can I become more receptive to God, to the Christ, to the spiritual influence?' The answer to that lies in increasing your givingness. Receptivity is attained only through giving. What you have to give is an individual matter with you. . . .

"Receptivity is the secret of spiritual attainment and receptivity is attained through givingness. If we have a little change or more to give, let us share it where we will, but remember that the givingness of which we speak is not as material as it is spiritual. The real givingness must be forgiveness, benevolence, peace, goodwill toward men. This is the givingness: goodwill toward men, setting free, holding no one in condemnation.

"Receptivity is the ability to perceive, to discern the spiritual good in man, the ability to discern the spiritual good that is embodied in all parts of this universe through your receptivity, because the more of the Christ that you discern in another, the more of the Christ comes to light in you....The word is 'giv-ingness.' Give to the Christ; and give the Christ to the world.... When we have opened our consciousness to this presence of God and received It within us, then our function on earth is the giving of It to the world."

Joel S. Goldsmith, "Opening the Door to Me,"
The 1964 San Francisco Special Class.

Chapter Twelve

Christ Ascended

When the message of the Infinite Way became clear to me, I did not know what to do with it except to write the book, *The Infinite Way,* and have it published. Soon thereafter three people from Ohio, a mother, a father, and a son came to me for instruction. Then, twelve people came, and in seventeen years this message had encircled the globe.

After I had discovered for myself the law or way of God that had proved beneficial in my individual experience, I could share whatever I had learned with the few who had expressed an interest in what I had discovered, and they in turn have been able to bring the presence and power of God into their experience and have continued to carry the message further. By virtue of having imparted the little I had learned, I immediately knew more than I had known before.

So, too, if I can impart one or more of the specific principles responsible for this worldwide activity to you, you can bring those principles into your individual life and show forth some measure of spiritual fruitage. Someone will observe the change in your life and will want to know about it, and you will begin to impart what you know. In sharing even that little, you will then find that you know twice as much. In this way, through our united effort, eventually peace will be established on earth. It will not be merely an interval between wars; it will not be just putting our fleet in mothballs again until time to call it out. If peace is brought to earth spiritually, it will be because a whole new principle of life has been revealed and a whole new era of consciousness has been opened.

When most persons think of world peace, they are probably thinking in the same way that people have been thinking for centuries, which is that there will just be no war. This is not peace, nor is it the peace promised by the Christ. The peace that the Christ promised is a peace that this world cannot give, a peace that is not merely the product of putting up the sword.

The Christ Mission

The Hebrews made the mistake of believing that the Messiah was a man who had come to earth and was going to free them from Rome, and probably from the Jewish Sanhedrin as well, the organized religion that was oppressing them, taking from them in tithes, sacrifices, and gifts much more than it had a right to take. The Master made it clear that he had a kingdom, but that his kingdom was not of "this world."[1] This he further exemplified when he said, "My peace give I unto you: but not as the world giveth, give I unto you."[2]

If we expect to bring to the world the freedom we hope to bring to ourselves individually, we must not think in terms of freedom from some pain, some lack, or some form of sin. That is the peace the world can give. Then what are we seeking through a realization of spiritual power and spiritual presence? The answer must inevitably be that we are seeking the peace the world cannot give. We are seeking the kingdom that is not of this world. We do not think in terms of increasing our income, expanding our business, improving our health, or adding to our happiness. Before us always are the questions: What is this hidden kingdom? What is this unrevealed kingdom that the Master came to reveal? Why did the Master come to earth? What was the Master's mission on earth? What is it that enabled him to set up a ministry which, although it has not been fulfilled in two thousand years, still dominates the thought of all mankind?

Even though we do not know what "My kingdom" is or what "My peace" is, we are aware that that is the discovery we must make. No one else has brought a religious concept to the world that so holds men and women, not only those of the Occidental world, but the message of the Christ has a tremendous hold on the Oriental world. This is what men and women are striving toward. Even though they do not know what it is, there is an inner conviction that this is the message and the way, and the world is going to keep on stumbling until it finds it.

Seek Only to Reveal the Spiritual Kingdom

If we were to think, when called upon for help, "How can I reduce this fever? How can I remove this sickness? How can I heal this sin? How can I provide supply where there is none?" we would all be lost, and no help would be received by those who call upon us. The help that is received is in direct proportion to our realization that we are not seeking to give the peace the world can give; we are not seeking to increase the temporal kingdom or temporal power. Our function is to reveal the kingdom of God, to reveal "My peace," the spiritual peace, the Christ-peace. Our function is to reveal the law of God in operation and to reveal omnipresence.

As we abide in this, after having had a period for meditation, prayer, or treatment, having shut out this world and all of its problems, and having overcome our good humanhood which wants to see that everybody has peace, we are established within ourselves. Our function, the Christ-function, then is to reveal spiritual harmony, spiritual grace, an inner kingdom. This enables us to relax, to feel an inner stillness, quietness, and peace, and then comes the experience. It can be described only

as a transcendental experience, because it transcends anything
that we can think of humanly, but it leaves us with a feeling that
God is on the scene and all is well. Then something does happen in the experience of those who have asked for help, something tangible on the human plane.

So far I have not met any students who have discovered, any
more than I have, how this spiritual realization becomes tangible on the human plane. To me it is a mystery. I have watched
it for more than thirty years and can bear witness to the miracles that take place when this transcendental peace descends
upon me, this feeling of oneness with God and the awareness of
omnipresence. The attitude of the person asking for help, if he
would benefit to the utmost from this message, must be one of
seeking an awareness of God's presence, not material benefits.

"God is a spirit: and they that worship him must worship
him in Spirit and in truth."³ God must be worshiped, prayed to,
in spirit and in truth. This does away with all the ancient concepts of prayer. God is spirit. What then can we expect of God
except something spiritual? If we expect anything other than the
spiritual, we are praying amiss. God is spirit; God must be
prayed to spiritually, not humanly. Humanly we may be ill and
humanly we may want to get well. For how many thousands of
years has that kind of praying been used? We must finally accept
the truth that God is spirit and, therefore, we are seeking of the
spirit that which is spiritual: the inner kingdom; "My kingdom"; the Christ-kingdom. We seek only "My peace," the
Christ-peace, the Christ-harmony.

The Christ Is the Spirit of God in Man

The Hebrews mistakenly believed that the Messiah was to
be a man. But the Messiah is not a man: the Messiah is the son
of God, and the son of God dwells in you and in me, not in a
time two thousand years ago or in a place known as the Holy
Land. True, the Christ was there, but the Christ was also "before

Abraham was,"⁴ and the Christ will never leave us or forsake us. The Christ is not in time or space: the Christ is the son of God, and the son of God, the spirit of God, dwells in us. We become the child of God, however, only when we consciously know this truth.

When that truth becomes clear to us, we are ready to begin our spiritual journey, but we cannot begin our spiritual journey seriously until we have perceived that God is spirit. The son of God is not a man in time or space. It is the Spirit that indwells all time and all space, not only in the human world, but the animal world, the vegetable world, and the mineral world. Animals are not really beasts: there are no beasts. Those we call "beasts" and who act beastly in the animal world are but the product of what we have sent forth into expression, and the beastly nature changes when ours does. What the world considers beasts can become as gentle as our home pets, merely by coming under the influence of a person touched with this revelation.

Man is not evil. When a so-called evil man is brought under the influence of a person who has realized his divine sonship, a change takes place, such as took place in the experience of a man about to be executed for a crime he had committed. An appeal was made to the governor of the state to commute the sentence. In the appeal the attorney stated, "This is not the man who committed the crime: this is a different man, a man with a different consciousness. This is a man with a soul." The man's sentence was commuted. Much the same sort of thing occurred in Hawaii with a man who had been sentenced to life in prison for murder and who came under the influence of a spiritually attuned person. The attorney who had prosecuted the man and brought about his conviction turned around and became his attorney, stating, "This is not the man who was originally sentenced in this court: this is a man reborn."

When we begin to perceive the nature of God, the nature of prayer, and the nature of the Christ, our consciousness changes.

We, of ourselves, cannot change our consciousness: the truth will, but we must entertain the truth.

There is no such God as the world has been worshiping these last few thousand years. God is not a superhuman being that is withholding divine grace from this earth, and who, if we just say the right words, sacrifice, light candles, or engage in some other ritual, will give His grace to this earth. There is no such God. To understand the truth we must understand that God is spirit; God is not afar off; God is not to be worshiped in holy temples or holy mountains, because the kingdom of God is within. Until we accept this new understanding of God as spirit, which calls for a radical change of attitude or perspective, paying lip service to it will not do it, nor will affirming do it. It takes a great deal of silent meditation, even a silent wrangling with our own former beliefs, until we reach that place within our consciousness where we can sit in quietness and in confidence and be assured: "The kingdom of God is where I am. Omnipresence means that God is where I am, here, within range of my own consciousness."

All of God is not limited to one individual. God sent forth His son in His own image and likeness, endowed with His spiritual power, ordained to heal the sick, to comfort, to supply, and to forgive the sinner. But that son of God is incarnated in me, in you, and in every "you" throughout this globe: the pagan, the atheist, the agnostic, the Christian, the Buddhist, the Vedantist. It makes no difference what his beliefs are. God is spirit, indivisible, inseparable from Himself, and therefore omnipresent in you, in every *you*.

Forgiveness of Sin, a Function of the Christ

By observing the ministry of Jesus Christ, who so completely showed forth his divine sonship, and which he said was within us, we can understand the function of the Christ, one of which is the forgiving of sin. For each of us, this is important.

In our human experience we have sinned greatly, and because most of our sins were committed ignorantly, we need not rehearse or rehash them.

Let us acknowledge, however, that as human beings we have strayed far from our Father's house, our Father's standard of conduct, and our Father's teaching. With this acknowledgment we are showing sufficient humility to take the next step and say, "Thank You, Father, that Your son, the Christ, the spirit of God in me, is here to forgive my sins. I carry within me my mediator, my meditation. I carry within my own consciousness the incarnated son of God whose function it is, when I ask for forgiveness, to give it."

Lip service will not suffice. This must be a once and for all confession: "Father, forgive me, I have not known what I have done. But now I know that Your son is incarnate within me, and one of Its functions is to forgive me my sins." Then the injunction is to go and sin no more and to watch each day that, to the highest extent possible, we do not violate the laws that we have come to know. Even so there will be more violations, but forgiveness "seventy times seven"[5] is still awaiting us. Our responsibility is to try our best to live up to whatever spiritual law we may now learn, and if we know that the Christ is not something in time or space, we have made a real beginning.

Healing as an Activity of the Christ

Another function of the Christ is to heal the sick. Why should we look outside for healing, when we have indwelling this principle of God, the law of God, the life of God, the son of God, the Christ who is ordained to heal the sick and to comfort? We have no longer left the Christ in the Holy Land of two thousand years ago. We have consciously established the Christ as incarnate within ourselves, embodied within us since "before Abraham was," and "unto the end of the world."[6] There is no longer a search for the Christ. Instead comes a recognition and an acknowledgment:

> The son of God dwells in me. The spiritual
> presence and power of God dwell in me, and that
> Presence is come that I might have life and
> that I might have life more abundantly.

It makes no difference that we have sinned. That has nothing to do with us. What has to do with us is that we have resurrected Christ from that tomb of two thousand years ago and have lifted him up within us. If the Christ be lifted up in us, we have the secret of a spiritually harmonious life, a peace that passes understanding, a peace that the honors, wealth, or glories of this world cannot give. We have a harmony, an abundance, a grace. This is true, however, only if the son of God be lifted up in us. So we lift up that son of God out of Jerusalem, out of the tomb of two thousand years ago, and raise Him up in our own consciousness, and there realize the presence of God in us, and Its function: "I am come that they might have life, and that they might have it more abundantly."[7]

No Idolatry in Any Form

In our meditations it is important to listen, because the Christ that is raised up in us will speak to us: in words sometimes, in an awareness other times—always in some understandable way. This is the reason the path of the Infinite Way calls for so many periods of meditation—short ones, just long enough to raise up the son of God in us, so that we have, not only the possibility, but the constant experience of inner communion. Then we can commune at will with the son of God, driving our car, doing housework, at business. The son of God is not confined to time or space: we can commune at any time that we can go within.

One thing is very important: there must be no idol worship. We must not have any pictures in our mind of God or the Christ, nor must we have any preconceived ideas as to the way the Christ will manifest in our experience. The human mind has been trained in the direction of idolatry, from the olden days when amulets and charms were endowed with special power to these modern days when crucifixes and stars are used. There has always been something to hold onto.

Metaphysics has its form of idolatry, too, substituting thoughts for things: "Send me a good thought" or "Hold a good thought for me." That practice would turn God into a thought or is an attempt to make a thought God. Blessings are ours in proportion as we can release ourselves from the bondage of thought. "Which of you by taking thought can add one cubit unto his stature?. . . Thou canst not make one hair white or black."[8] If we cannot, by taking thought, do these little things, how much we can do with thought insofar as the big ones are concerned?

It is not thought that accomplishes the things of the world, certainly not your thoughts or my thoughts. The thoughts that are imparted to us from within, they are power. "The word of God is quick, and powerful, and sharper than any two-edged sword."[9] Those who develop the ability to find an inner stillness receive the word of God. In fact, it is the word of God that makes up all the great mystical messages that have ever been given to man. None of these was invented by man. Different messages in different parts of the world at different times, coming through persons who never had the opportunity of knowing one another, reveal that they have all heard the still, small voice and all received the same assurance: "My peace give I unto you: not as the world giveth." It is a different kind of peace. Therefore, when we go within, we do not outline the kind of peace we want or the kind of kingdom we wish manifested, because we are seeking for a hidden kingdom, a hidden Grace, known not to "man, whose breath is in his nostrils."[10] Yet, when we attain it, the conditions of our outer life automatically change.

Lifting Up the Son of God in Everyone Makes Us One With All Life

The son of God which we have raised up in us is in every individual. When we are one with the spiritual center of our being, we are one with the spiritual essence of all that exists everywhere on the face of the globe, everywhere, and in the spaces beyond. When we are consciously one with the Spirit within, we are consciously one with the Spirit that animates everyone everywhere: human, animal, vegetable, mineral. That includes not only this earth, but all the planets that are beyond this one, because Spirit is not limited to earth. Spirit is the essence, the substance, and the law behind all creation everywhere, and we become one with It only when we become one with our own center, with this risen Christ in us.

As we lift up the Christ in us, we remove the Christ from time and space, and realize It as an activity of our consciousness, a substance, a law, the spirit of God within us. Then we are one with all being, and we are one with all life: life of every nature, and life on any and every plane. We are one with the creative genius of the world: the inventive, artistic, and musical genius. We will not show forth all of these in our individual experience, very few do, but we will show forth the one that is meant for our individual expression.

Bringing the Spiritual Presence to the World

As we begin to experience human good as a direct result of our spiritual contact, we are in that same measure bringing that spiritual presence to the entire world. Only in this way can the kingdom of God come to earth. We pray in the Lord's Prayer, "Thy will be done in earth,"[11] but that will is not being done very much, is it? Is there any country where we can say the will of God is very much in evidence? The will of God is not in the earthquake; the will of God is not in war; the will of God is not in death. God has no pleasure in our dying: "For I have no pleasure in the death of him that dieth, saith the Lord God: wherefore turn yourselves, and live ye."[12] God is not in disease; God is not in the evils of this world; and because we see so much evil prevalent in the world, we know that there is not yet too much of God's will being done on earth.

When will God's kingdom come and His will be done on earth? When? First must come the demonstration of it in some measure in our personal experience. We cannot demonstrate it for anyone until, in some measure, we have demonstrated it for ourselves. The moment we have demonstrated for ourselves some measure of the kingdom of God, it will not be long before one or more come and ask, "How? Why? Where? When?" Then, as we begin to impart—and let us be sure that we impart only the tiny little bit that we have proved—we will discover that in that imparting our own wisdom is increasing.

God Cannot Be Known With the Mind

God is nothing objective to us. Therefore, we cannot have a thought about God that could be God. There is no way of our knowing God with the mind. The closest we come to God is when we have no thought about God, but can pray, "Enlighten me." There is no God at all that we could think of up in our mind. God is subjective. No thought about God is God.

The closer we come to the truth that God *is,* the closer we come to the God-experience. God *is.* From deep down within, there wells up the experience of God. We might think of it as God announcing Itself, God revealing Itself. Then we will know that we have seen God face to face, but only when all efforts to think have been overcome, because just as God cannot be made into an image externally, so God cannot be imaged internally.

The one creating the image is the creator; therefore, nothing that the creator can create would be God. It is like saying that no truth in a book is Truth, and it is not, because the truth in a book is the truth about the Truth. God is Truth. Can God be squeezed into a book? It is when God is uttering Itself that Truth is being expressed, and only God can express God. Only Truth can express Truth. Not even a man can do that, or a woman. That has to be from way down inside, and when It comes through, It surprises the hearer, even the one through whom It is coming, because no man ever invented Truth; no man ever wrote Truth.

Truth utters Itself, and in proportion to our ability to be still, to have no preconceived opinions or theories, and to be willing to let It reveal Itself, any of us can be instruments through which It utters Itself. If it takes a little time, it is worth it. It is really worthwhile to learn about "My kingdom" and "My peace." It is a realm unknown to human beings, except those who have transcended their humanness enough to be still and hear that voice.

The Christ Is Born in the Manger of Human Consciousness

Were it not for the still small voice uttering Itself, we would not know today that the Christ was not a man twenty centuries ago, but that the Christ is the spirit in us. It is only because it has been voiced again and again through the ages, and is being voiced today, that we now have this gift of the Son, born in a manger, born in the manger of our humanhood, as lowly a place as can ever be discovered. Only as the Christ is born in us do we realize how completely nothing we are without It, and then we realize that "I can of mine own self do nothing. . . . If I bear witness of myself, my witness is not true."[13] It is the indwelling spirit, that which Paul called "the Christ," that which Jesus called "the Father within," that does the work.

We can only know the function of the son of God by going through the New Testament again and understanding the work the man Jesus performed: forgiving the sinner, healing the sick, feeding the hungry, comforting those that mourn. Through this, we discover the function of the son of God in us. It is there for that same purpose. It has been there the same length of time: since "before Abraham was." It will be there the same length of time: "unto the end of the world."

We should live with this son of God, commune with the son of God, be grateful that out of all this world we have learned, and should very soon be demonstrating, that the son of God is alive, resurrected out of the tomb of Jerusalem, and ascended up into our consciousness, there to be the mediator between us and God, the point of contact, the point of communion, and point of prayer, the point of realization.

The Indwelling Presence in Everyone

Beautiful healings may take place, and some years later there may be a relapse. Then we get a letter asking, "Why?" In every such case that I have ever seen, the answer is the same. The person forgot to "sin no more, lest a worse thing come unto [him]."[14] He went right back to the same human state of consciousness in which originally he was living, and what can it bring forth?

But what control we can have over our own lives once we know sin, disease, and death do not come from God! They are the externalization of human consciousness. If we want less of sin, disease, and death in our experience, then our consciousness must become less human and more divine. That comes about only by raising up the Christ in ourselves, and letting It bring about a transformation of our consciousness.

If you or I had the power to release every person from his hospital bed this night or every man or woman in prison from prison, we need not think we would be doing anything so very great. It is only in proportion as our realization of the risen Christ *transforms* the consciousness of an individual that that individual has something for which to thank us.

Let us remember that the presence indwells every one of us, and our recognition of it is helping to awaken It in the rest of mankind. Just as a person, recognizing the indwelling Christ, brings transformation into the experience of another person, so should we be able to conceive of the contribution all of us together, dwelling and recognizing this raised up Christ in human consciousness throughout the world, will make to world peace. That peace passes understanding; it is the real peace, because it is a peace that will change the consciousness of man. This is the only real blessing there is.

ACROSS THE DESK

What does Christmas mean to you? Is it an experience completely out here in the world, just a busy time to participate in a series of festivities? For many, this is true, and Christmas has lost its real meaning as an experience of consciousness.

This Christmas, let us set aside time to contemplate the real meaning of Christmas as our awakening to the Christ-presence that It may be raised up in us and we may become instruments of Its activity.

To each of you, the joys of this special time, but above all, a deeper awareness of Christmas as an activity of consciousness.

TAPE RECORDED EXCERPTS
Prepared by the Editor

Students often wonder why some problems are met so quickly and others seem so difficult to see through or why the same problem yields so quickly in one student and so slowly or not at all in another. Joel usually indicates that the sole responsibility for healing rests with the practitioner. Yet on other occasions he has maintained that some students are so engulfed in material sense that no healing takes place. How can these two apparently contradictory statements be reconciled? The excerpt following will clear up any seeming contradiction and help to clarify the reason for a lack of healing:

"Is Lack of Healing Always a Failure?"

"When the Infinite Way teaches that the healer alone must accept the responsibility for healing, it does not mean that the practitioner should give you a written guarantee that you are going to be healed in spite of anything that you may do to stop it. What it means is this: If you ask me for help, I must assume the responsibility of bringing out that healing because I am the one who is supposed to have the spiritual understanding, not the patient. If the patient had it, he would not have asked me for help. Therefore it is my responsibility. . . to do the work. . . "Because I've taken that responsibility. . . doesn't mean that you can't stop the healing from taking place. It doesn't mean for a minute that every healing is going to take place. It only means that I'm not going to say to you, 'Now if you were a little more loving,' or 'If you were more grateful,' or 'If you read four more pages every day of my book. . . .' I'm not going to put that responsibility on you. I am going to take the same responsibility when you call on me that I would have to take if you called on me to help your pet dog. I could not ask the dog to go to church regularly or to read so many pages of scripture or to hold the right thoughts or to be more moral or grateful.

"None of those things must be permitted to enter the question of spiritual healing. If you ask for help for someone who is unconscious or dying, how can I turn to him and ask him to cooperate? It is impossible. I must accept the responsibility for doing the work. But I cannot be responsible if the healing does not take place. I am only responsible for giving my utmost to it in all faithfulness and with all integrity.

"There may be many reasons why healings do not take place. You only need turn to Jesus and his disciples to wonder what prevented Jesus from healing Judas of whatever greed or lust was handling him or what prevented Jesus from healing Peter, and. . . you will know that nobody can be responsible for healing everybody. . . . For example, you are an individual, and if you decide that you want to cling to your materialism, lust, greed, animality, you have that right, and nobody can break through. That's your part of it.

"But the practitioner's part is to accept the responsibility for doing the work and not evade it by saying, 'Well, of course, you're not a member of our group. That makes it more difficult,' or, 'You're not grateful'; or, 'Well, I've heard that you're immoral.' All of that goes for nothing, and no one should indulge that in the Infinite Way.

"Accept the responsibility to take over the work, do it, and stand on your work. If something happens that looks like failure, don't believe that either, because actually that which the world calls death itself is not failure. If it were so, then Jesus failed, and Paul and John, and all the great spiritual lights, for they have all left this plane of consciousness. No, death is not always a failure. Sometimes the passing from this scene is a part of our very demonstration.

"That, you cannot believe until you catch a vision of what eternal life means and of God unfolding as individual consciousness. And then you realize how to rise step by step from infancy to youth, from youth to young manhood and womanhood, and to maturity, . . . and keep on. . . until we keep right on walking out of this plane. Do not judge after appearances. Do not be too quick. Stephen was stoned to death. That apparently would be considered a failure. Who is to say that that was a failure for Stephen? . . . Don't judge that way. Judge righteous judgment, and it maybe given you to perceive how we evolve from one state of consciousness to another."

Joel S. Goldsmith, "Protective Work As It Should Be," *The 1958 London Closed Class.*

About the Series

The 1971 through 1981 *Letters* will be published as a series of eleven fine-quality soft cover books. Each book published in the first edition will be offered by Acropolis Books and The Valor Foundation, and can be ordered from either source:

ACROPOLIS BOOKS, INC.
8601 Dunwoody Place
Suite 303
Atlanta, GA 30350-2509
(800) 773-9923
acropolisbooks@mindspring.com

THE VALOR FOUNDATION
1101 Hillcrest Drive
Hollywood, FL 33021
(954) 989-3000
info@valorfoundation.com

Scriptural References and Notes

CHAPTER ONE

1. Revelation 21:27.
2. Jeremiah 8:22.
3. Matthew 4:4.
4. John 18:36.
5. John 10:10.
6. Philippians 4:13.
7. Hebrews 13:5.
8. John 14:27.
9. John 8:11.
10. Luke 7:48.
11. I Corinthians 3:16.
12. I Corinthians 6:19.
13. I Kings 19:12.
14. I Thessalonians 5:17.
15. Matthew 6:19.
16. II Corinthians 5:1.
17. John 11:25.
18. John 10:30.
19. John 15:4.
20. Matthew 6:33.

CHAPTER TWO

1. Matthew 5:39.
2. Matthew 26:52.
3. Matthew 7:14.
4. John 8:58.
5. Matthew 28:20.
6. Hebrews 13:5.
7. II Chronicles 20:15,17.
8. John 8:32.
9. John 7:24.
10. Matthew 23:9.
11. I Corinthians 15:31.
12. Luke 17:21.
13. John 5:31.
14. John 10:30.
15. John 14:10.
16. Luke 17:21.
17. I Kings 19:12.
18. II Corinthians 12:2.
19. I Corinthians 2:14.
20. Romans 8:17.
21. Matthew 7:14.

CHAPTER THREE

1. Galatians 6:8.
2. John 10:30.
3. John 10:29.
4. I Corinthians 3:16.
5. Matthew 6:19.
6. Isaiah 2:22.
7. Galatians 2:20.
8. John 18:36.
9. II Corinthians 12:9.

CHAPTER FOUR

1. John 4:24.
2. Matthew 5:11.
3. Matthew 4:4.
4. James 5:16.
5. John 18:36.
6. John 14:27.
7. Matthew 4:19.
8. Matthew 10:37.
9. Matthew 6:10.
10. Exodus 3:5.
11. Isaiah 55:1.
12. Matthew 16:16.
13. Matthew 16:17.
14. Galatians 6:8.
15. John 4:32.
16. Isaiah 2:22.
17. Matthew 6:20.
18. John 10:30.
19. I Corinthians 13:12.
20. Zechariah 4:6.

CHAPTER FIVE

1. Romans 8:7.
2. Matthew 5:38,39.
3. I Corinthians 15:31.
4. I Kings 19:12.
5. Robert Browning.
6. Psalm 46:10.
7. Luke 15:31
8. Hebrews 13:5.
9. Hebrews 11:34.
10. John 16:33.
11. Isaiah 45:2.
12. John 14:2.
13. Isaiah 30:15.
14. Zechariah 4:6.
15. Psalm 127:1.
16. Galatians 2:20.
17. John 5:30.
18. John 14:10.
19. John 10:30.
20. John 14:28.
21. Acts 10:34.
22. Matthew 5:44,46.
23. Matthew 5:23,24.
24. Isaiah 2:22.
25. Matthew 22:39.
26. Matthew 25:40.
27. Matthew 25:45.
28. Psalm 127:1.
29. Job 23:14.
30. Psalm 138:8.

CHAPTER SIX

1. John 8:32.
2. I Thessalonians 5:17.
3. Proverbs 3:6.
4. Psalm 24:1.
5. Psalm 127:1.
6. Matthew 22:37.
7. John 6:35.
8. Romans 8:38,39.
9. Hebrews 11:34.
10. John 19:11.
11. John 7:24.
12. Isaiah 65:24.
13. Acts 10:34.
14. Exodus 3:5.
15. Psalm 91:7.
16. Luke 15:31.
17. Isaiah 26:3.

CHAPTER SEVEN

1. Matthew 9:6.
2. John 9:6.
3. John 11:43.
4. II Chronicles 32:8.
5. Romans 8:7.
6. Luke 17:21.
7. Isaiah 44:8.
8. By the author.
9. By the author.
10. See the author's *The Infinite Way Letters 1958.* [Currently out of print].
11. Revelation 21:27.
12. Isaiah 2:22.
13. Psalm 23:4.
14. John 8:32.
15. Acts 10:34.
16. Luke 4:8.

CHAPTER EIGHT

1. Luke 12:30,32.
2. Isaiah 2:22.
3. John 15:13.
4. Matthew 6:4.
5. Acts 10:34.
6. By the author (Acropolis Books, Atlanta, 1997).
7. By the author (Acropolis Books, Atlanta, 1997).
8. John 10:30.
9. Isaiah 45:2.

CHAPTER NINE

1. Exodus 3:14.
2. By the author, *The Infinite Way.*
3. Joel 2:25.
4. John 10:10.
5. John 12:45.
6. Matthew 23:9.
7. John 8:32.
8. Acts 5:5-10.
9. John 14:6.
10. Matthew 28:20.
11. John 10:30.

CHAPTER TEN

1. II Corinthians 3:17.
2. Psalm 23:4.
3. Luke 17:21.
4. Romans 8:5,7.
5. Psalm 139:7.
6. Hebrews 13:5.
7. Exodus 3:5.
8. Deuteronomy 33:27.
9. I Samuel 3:9.
10. I Kings 19:12.
11. Isaiah 45:2.
12. John 14:2.
13. John 19:11.
14. Isaiah 33:22.
15. John 8:32.
16. Matthew 5:25.
17. Luke 12:29.
18. Philippians 2:5.

CHAPTER ELEVEN

1. John 5:30.
2. Philippians 2:5.
3. Matthew 26:42.
4. Matthew 5:39.
5. Luke 10:20.
6. Acts 20:24.
7. II Chronicles 32:8.
8. Luke 17:21.
9. Psalm 42:11.
10. Acts 10:34.
11. Psalm 24:1.
12. Luke 15:31.
13. James 5:16.
14. Psalm 91:7.
15. Matthew 23:37.
16. Exodus 3:5.
17. Romans 8:17.

CHAPTER TWELVE

1. John 18:36.
2. John 14:27.
3. John 4:24.
4. John 8:58.
5. Matthew 18:22.
6. Matthew 28:20.
7. John 10:10.
8. Matthew 5:36.
9. Hebrews 4:12.
10. Isaiah 2:22.
11. Matthew 6:10.
12. Ezekiel 18:32.
13. John 5:30,31.
14. John 5:14.

Joel Goldsmith
Tape Recorded Classes
Corresponding to the
Chapters of this Volume

Tape recordings may be ordered from

THE INFINITE WAY
PO Box 2089, Peoria AZ 85380-2089
Telephone 800-922-3195 Fax 623-412-8766

E-mail: infiniteway@earthlink.net
www.joelgoldsmith.com
Free Catalog Upon Request